# Diversity
## and the
# Bottom Line:

## PROSPERING IN THE GLOBAL ECONOMY

TurnKey
press

# by Pamela K. Henry

Library of Congress Cataloging-in-publication Data

Henry, Pamela K.
Diversity and the Bottom Line

p.    cm.    includes notes    includes bibliography


1. Diversity in Workplace  2. Organizational Change
3. Corporate Culture  4. Management

I. Title  II. Author  III. Business  IV. Monograph

ISBN:  0-9740030-1-8

658.3 HE    HF 5549.5          LC

First Edition: May 2003


Published in the United States by

**TurnKey**
**press**

2525 West Anderson Lane, Suite 540
Austin, Texas 78757
Tel: 512.407.8876
Fax: 512.478.2117
E-mail: info@turnkeypress.com
Web: www.turnkeypress.com

Cover design by M.J. Wetherhead

*With Love*
*to*
*Nate, Grace and Faith*


*May your uniqueness, wisdom and humanity*
*be ever nourished in a world committed to honoring the nobility*
*of the human spirit and the power of difference*

# ACKNOWLEDGMENTS

My deepest appreciation goes to best friend and partner, Joe Kolly, for his constant support and encouragement during this project.

I want to thank my wonderful family. First, my mother, Ginny Bull, for her steadfast love and belief in me over the years. Secondly, my jewel of a daughter, Erica Leake, for choosing and living the values that nurture and enrich my life every day as well as those around her. Thirdly, to my brother, David Kenneally, whose encouragement and humor has always helped me stay the course. Last but not least, to my father, who inspired me during his lifetime to be compassionate and make a difference.

I am indebted to many friends and colleagues for their continued support. In particular, I want to thank Eun Kim, Linda Escamilla, Rosanna Riffle, Mickey Michaels and Barbara Santos for providing insight and wisdom to my work. My work is richer and better because of their inputs. My appreciation also goes to Steve Leven, Carolyn Leighton, Dr. William Wulf, Dr. Edward Hubbard and Anne Berry Shindell for reviewing my book.

I am grateful to M.J. Wetherhead for her beautiful creativity in designing my cover and her steadfast encouragement and to Ryan Myers for his superb layout design.

I want to thank Cathy Miller and the staff of the Small Business Development Center for their assistance in providing valuable research.

Finally, I am indebted to the work of Mindy Reed, my editor, who not only helped to shape this work, but who also understands diversity and champions it every day in her life.

# ABOUT the AUTHOR

Pamela K. Henry is an organizational development specialist whose speaking and consulting practice includes expertise in the areas of Global Diversity, Talent Management and EEO and Compliance. Pamela has over twenty years experience with two Fortune 500 companies and has served on numerous national and community-based boards.

She has a broad array of competencies with proven skills in building interpersonal business relationships, client management and optimizing the performance and effectiveness of organizations.

Pamela's extensive background includes seven years with Motorola designing the framework and strategies for implementation of a sustainable diversity initiative and its integration throughout the businesses to support organizational goals of attracting, developing and retaining a best-in-class multicultural workforce. This effort included development of infrastructure, metrics, marketing and communication plans. She was also a lead architect of Motorola's sourcing strategies designed to attract a diverse pipeline of executive talent. She served as Regional Manager for Motorola's Southwest and Western regions.

During her successful fourteen-year career with Texas Instruments, Pamela led various functions of Human Resources, including EEO and compliance; staffing & restructuring; employee relations; compliance, and employee communications. Pamela's career with TI culminated in her selection as one of five managers asked to serve full-time on its Corporate Human Resources

Reengineering Team, a two-year assignment that focused on process redesign of key HR services and implementation of streamlined systems and deliverables.

In support of her passion for diversity and continuous learning about cultures, she has traveled extensively in the U.S., United Kingdom, Europe, Mexico, Canada, Greece and Turkey. Pamela has written articles on organizational change and effective diversity recruitment practices. She is recognized as an excellent speaker and workshop facilitator on diversity and multiculturalism.

Pamela holds two bachelors' degrees and a Masters degree in Counseling.


Pamela K. Henry & Associates
13329 Kingman Drive, Suite B
Austin, Texas 78729
(512) 335-1237
www.pamelakhenry.com

# PREFACE

## WHAT THIS BOOK IS NOT ABOUT

There have been significant research studies and many excellent books written about why diversity is "the right thing to do." They espouse the moral and socially responsible reasons why organizations, their leaders and employees should be committed to a movement that values diversity, ameliorates oppression and creates equal opportunity. I embrace these arguments and honor the seminal work done by such luminaries in diversity as R. Roosevelt Thomas, Barbara Loden, Gardenswartz and Rowe, Judith Katz, John Fernandez, Peggy McIntosh, Ann Morrison and many others.

However, that is not what this book is about. I have chosen to present diversity in a much less philosophical and more pragmatic manner, using a bottom-line approach that will appeal to business and other leaders, with the intent of transforming their commitment to diversity into action. Why? Because their organizations will be much more successful and much wealthier with diversity as their *competitive advantage*.

Very little has been written about the bottom-line impacts of diversity – how companies can actually improve business results such as productivity, creativity and profitability by incorporating diversity into how they conduct business. There are forces occurring in the U.S. and globally that pose great challenge to companies doing business today. The world is the *new business unit*, and *diversity has become a requirement* for companies to be successful going forward in a global economy. These are the issues that challenge business leaders today – their *call to action* – and why this book has been written.

# WHO SHOULD READ THIS BOOK

For over a decade I designed framework and implemented strategies in support of diversity initiatives for Fortune 500 companies. I have consistently been asked the question, "OK. I understand why my support of diversity is important, but what *IS* the business case for diversity?" Read this book, and you shall know the answer!

## This book is written for all who want to improve organizational climate and instill inclusion-based practices. Specifically,

1. Leaders and managers of companies and other organizations where diversity initiatives have been implemented, are being planned or where the seeds for such actions need to be planted. This book will help them understand the business reasons for diversity, articulate this rationale in a comprehensive and compelling fashion and act upon it.

2. Diversity practitioners, task forces and employee resource groups who are championing diversity in their organizations will find valuable strategies and practical tools that will enhance their ability to implement and sustain a diversity initiative.

I have divided this book into two parts. The first presents the arguments that support the strong correlation between diversity and the bottom line. I have identified ten business imperatives that tie diversity to achieving greater profitability.

The second part of the book includes helpful frameworks, strategies, metrics and tools to assist organizations with the implementation of their diversity initiative.

While the primary focus is on Corporate America, this book will be valuable to leaders of companies in other countries who want to better understand diversity; national professional/business associations; non-profit organizations; universities (particularly those with MBA and diversity programs); libraries; government agencies; the military; and small and medium-sized businesses.

# CONTENTS

## PART I:
# THE BUSINESS CASE FOR DIVERSITY

# PART II:
# STRATEGIES AND TOOLS

# INTRODUCTION:

# WHY DIVERSITY IS GOOD FOR BUSINESS

No matter who you are, you're going to have to work with people who are different from you. You're going to have to sell to people who are different from you, and buy from people who are different from you, and manage people who are different from you. This is how we do business. If it's not your destination, you should get off the plane now.

> -   Ted Childs, Vice-President
>     Global Workforce Diversity
>     IBM[1]

1

## THE SEEDS OF DIVERSITY IN AMERICA

Few countries are as diverse as America. Throughout our history, peoples from different lands and regions of the world have headed for our shores. They brought with them their cultures, traditions, languages and religions. As we have grappled with the challenges that a multicultural society presents, it has sometimes felt as if the rest of the world has been an observer, taking side bets as to how our grand experiments in social justice, fairness and equal opportunity would turn out.

America's heritage of diversity gives us a *richness, strength* and *advantage* few other nations on Earth will ever know. Success in developing a harmonious, thriving multicultural society will offer the U.S. another avenue for global leadership.

Diversity is an essential component of any civil society. It's more than a moral imperative; it is a *global necessity.*

## FROM SOCIAL JUSTICE TO VALUING DIFFERENCES

In the days of affirmative action, the focus was limited to offering access to the workplace primarily to people of color and women. It was viewed as a moral and social responsibility that would make up for past wrongdoing. A company was expected to open its doors, if only a little, to these new entrants, with no further obligation. If beneficiaries of affirmative action had difficulty fitting in to the culture and being assimilated, there was obviously something wrong with them.

Several decades and many lawsuits later, companies began to look inwardly to try and understand why *they*, people of color and women, seemed to be having such difficulty at work. "After all," the argument went, "*we* didn't experience this difficulty. We persevered and succeeded. They're just not trying hard enough. They have a bad case of entitlement."

Meantime, the careers of these new entrants stalled, and they began leaving companies. Some voluntarily, some not so voluntarily. Complaints included that employees were never given an opportunity and never had visibility to upper management or the "unwritten rules." People of color and women became more vocal in their frustration. Companies began asking themselves, "why don't our systems work for these people?" *And a voice cried out, it's the culture!*

From this shared frustration, the diversity movement was born. Diversity proponents maintained, if a company focuses on creating a culture that is trusting, respecting and *valuing* of women and people of color, its ability to recruit and retain diverse talent and foster a reputation of being an "employer of choice" will be enhanced. Affirmative action tended to cause polarization and backlash. They began focusing on an *inclusive* culture; one that went beyond being culture-specific in recognizing only women and people of color, to a multicultural perspective that included less visible, more intrinsic differences. They have been continuously expanding the definition of diversity ever since, striving to cover any possible dimension of diversity so that no one would be left out, not even white males.

The primary focus of the diversity movement has been on training to raise awareness about valuing differences and embracing the contributions that multiple perspectives bring to the workplace. While companies proudly tout their diversity initiatives and networking groups through cultural events and celebrations, the events rarely tie into business practices.

Something is missing. It's as if the heart and soul of the company have checked out, and only the lips are moving. Common complaints include:

- "I feel like I'm sitting on the bench waiting to be called into the game."
- "I was hired as a token and am exploited by it."
- "My suggestions and recommendations are ignored by my manager and colleagues."
- "I am expected to be the spokesperson for my *group*. Why? Whites don't have to speak for their group."
- "I feel like I have to act white in order to be taken seriously."
- "Why does the environment still feel so paternalistic?"
- "Why do the same barriers exist that existed at the vanguard of affirmative action?"

Diversity needs to be thought of as the *fabric* of an organization, weaving the uniqueness of difference into the organizational culture. The "melting pot" theory of assimilation, where individuals were expected to conform to the norms of the dominant culture to fit in, no longer applies. Employees should not have to deny their differences to get ahead. The energy wasted by individuals trying to "fit in" to a culture that does not recognize or accept their differences, negatively impacts productivity and morale of an organization. People with differences are marginalized. And their competency continues to be questioned.

I don't disagree with what companies have tried to do with diversity initiatives. The corporate culture needs to be inclusive, now more than ever. It needs to appeal to as many constituencies as possible. Still, we haven't gone *far enough* to leverage the power of diversity and the vast opportunities in process, productivity and profit that it offers business.

It is pure pragmatism to treat diversity as an asset, as a way of doing business. Diversity needs to be aligned with other business strategies, because it impacts the bottom line just as much as they do, especially now. Acknowledging and integrating new and meaningful ways to do work that a diverse representation contributes is one enabling strategy.

## THE BUSINESS CASE FOR DIVERSITY

In an insightful article in the *Harvard Business Review* entitled, "Making Differences Matter: A New Paradigm for Managing Diversity,"[2] David Thomas and Robin Ely argue that linking the definition of diversity to the actual doing of work has led to improved performance in companies. Of the organizations that they studied, a common "*aha*" experience for the leaders involved was that increasing diversity alone did not enhance organizational effectiveness and productivity. It was what they did to incorporate these differences, diverse experiences and ways of doing tasks into the fabric of the organization that led to breakthrough performance. They found that going beyond the traditional margins of diversity and incorporating cultural competencies into actual work processes was far more effective.

Take ethnic marketing, for example. In a prior life one of these companies would likely have given the African-American market here in the U.S. to an African-American employee and the market in Mexico to a Latino. Now, when that same company is developing an ethnic marketing strategy, it ensures that the planning team has multidimensional diversity represented in strategic planning and decision-making at the initial stages. Their experience with the culture(s) being addressed is not only valued, it's *demanded*, in order to optimize the success of the project. Why? Because the purchasing decisions of the company's customers are demanding it.

It is no longer good enough to *tolerate* differences; we must *look for* differences. As futurist, Jajoda Perich-Anderson[3] believes, organizations need to develop a "fascination with difference." A focus on differences allows that company to learn, increase innovation, grow and become more profitable.

Once a company goes beyond thinking about diversity only in terms of how a person looks and where he or she comes from, it can begin thinking of diversity in a more holistic fashion.

Seeking and incorporating differences in how people think and work is essential to the culture of an organization if it wants to be able to team effectively and win in a global economy. So, it's not just about the culture. *It's also about the bottom line.*

The connection between diversity and shareholder value was first made in the 1994 Glass Ceiling Commission Report.[4] It found that the annualized rate of Return on Investment (ROI) for the 100 companies with the lowest ra-tings in diversity and equal opportunity factors averaged 7.9%, compared to 18.3% for the 100 companies rated the highest.

In a 1999 *Fortune* article, the case was made that the ten Best Companies for Minorities to Work For all matched or beat the S&P 500 in returns over the previous five years.[5]

Demonstrating an absolute link between a diversity-friendly culture and profitability is a challenging proposition. Why? Because, while there is fairly compelling theoretical data for the connection, there is no insurmountable evidence that diversity, and not some other factor(s), is the primary contributor of a positive ROI. It appears intuition rather than statistics drives the argument. Yet, as Ann Morrison points out, diversity is not unique in this regard:

> What direct evidence do we have that better customer service is directly related to the bottom line? Do we know for sure that product quality increases profits more than clever advertising?... Businesses operate on a host of assumptions ... but few can be conclusively proved. The lack of a guarantee is hardly an excuse for not taking action.[6]

So, the question becomes, should diversity be held to a higher standard than other company initiatives which also lack metrics that make a direct correlation to successful results?

Like other business initiatives, diversity is not conducted in a vacuum. Attributing positive bottom line effects specifically to a diversity initiative is not easy. However, this dilemma is also true of other organizational programs such as strategic off-site meetings held for the purpose of boosting morale, product development, teamwork or sales, the effects of which are rarely measured. Yet, they continue to receive sponsorship from top management.

## DIVERSITY AND THE BOTTOM LINE

The demographics speak for themselves. The ethnic and multicultural customer base domestically and globally is increasingly diverse. Today, multicultural groups comprise over 30% of the U.S. population. By 2050, half of the U.S. population will be multicultural. Globally, 99% of the population growth is occurring in three regions: Africa, Asia and Latin America, all three comprised of diverse peoples.

This emerging customer base is growing, both in strength and wealth. In the U.S., Latinos, African-Americans and Asian-Americans control more than $1.3 trillion dollars in purchasing power. Older Americans, people with disabilities and gays and lesbians control another $1.6 trillion. The multicultural market in the U.S. is outpacing and outspending the mainstream market, growing 65% faster. Women own over 8 million businesses in the U.S. People of color own 3 million. These businesses are potential suppliers and customers.

With a growth rate of 5%, by 2010 the emerging markets of Eastern Europe, Asia (excluding Japan and China) and Latin America will equal the purchasing power of the U.S. and Western Europe. Yet, few U.S. companies recognize the changing complexion of the American and global consumers. These markets are ignored and untapped. Companies are missing out on a **huge** opportunity to grow market share and positively impact their bottom line. To capitalize on these markets, I believe there are two strategies that need to be adopted by enterprising companies that want to create competitive advantage through diversity.

First, they need to commit to conducting *global intelligence* and acquiring *cultural competence* on an ongoing basis to more effectively deal with these new customers, domestically and globally.

Second, they need to begin *diversifying their employee base* to better relate to the emerging marketplace. To achieve optimum financial results for the company, this strategy must include developing a *reverence for work experiences, habits and processes of diverse employees* and including their knowledge and skills in designing, manufacturing, marketing, selling and servicing to the emerging multicultural markets.

Opportunities in the ethnic global and domestic markets can be directly translated to ROI and profitability through increased sales and an expanded customer base. There are other benefits of treating diversity as a business advantage to the bottom line. They include:

- Higher creativity and productivity, which result in more patents and innovation.
- A greater array of products having increased functionality that appeal to a broader consumer base.
- Greater access to a wider talent pool anywhere in the world
- Continuity of knowledge, experience, skills and intellectual capital due to improved retention.
- A greater selection of suppliers with a lower cost structure.
- Mergers and acquisitions that are successful and long-lived.
- An enhanced image in the community with positive impact to market share.
- Increased shareholders and stock price.

## THE JOURNEY BEGINS....MAKING THE CASE:

As we begin our journey of exploring the business imperatives, which will underscore the strong correlation between diversity and the bottom line, let's assume some roles.

You are the CEO of a Fortune 500 company.

I will be your guide on this journey suggesting why you need to change the way you're doing business today and why you must do it *NOW*, or risk losing the opportunity to create greater success and profitability for your company.

You're skeptical about diversity. You've always felt a social responsibility to offer opportunities to everyone. Yet, you've never been able to make the connection between diversity and its benefits to business. When business conditions deteriorate, your intention "to do the right thing" has been replaced by a focus on reducing costs and stabilizing the business.

### A reality check reveals that:

- Your company is currently in trouble.

- You're experiencing high turnover (higher than your competitors).

- Your recruiting budget is out of control, and you're finding it more and more difficult to attract the candidates you need to get back on track.

- Product development is slowed, and shipping commitments are not being met. Customers are jumping ship.

- Productivity and creativity are languishing.

- Patents are down 25% from a year ago, and new product designs are not forthcoming.

- The organization is dysfunctional—teams aren't gelling and conflict is apparent.

- Overall execution is poor.

- You've just learned a major lawsuit has been filed against the company for alleged discrimination in promotion practices.

- The stock price is down, and analysts have not had very positive things to say.
- Shareholders and the Board of Directors are edgy.

You have a burning platform to implement some effective changes quickly. This journey will help you do that. To make it easier for you, I'll even provide you with summary highlights at the end of each chapter should you become bleary-eyed with all the persuasive facts I'm going to throw your way.

We have no time to waste! Let the journey begin...

## SUMMARY HIGHLIGHTS
## Introduction: Why Diversity is Good for Business

- The "melting pot" theory of assimilation, where individuals were expected to conform to the norms of the dominant culture to fit in, no longer applies.

- Once an organization goes beyond thinking about diversity only in terms of how a person looks and where he or she comes from, it can begin thinking of diversity in a more holistic fashion.

- The demographics speak for themselves. The ethnic and multicultural customer base domestically and globally is increasingly diverse.

- Companies are missing out on a huge opportunity to grow market share and positively impact their bottom line by ignoring multicultural constituencies globally and domestically.

- A commitment to conducting global intelligence and acquiring cultural competence on an ongoing basis will enable companies to more effectively deal with these new customers, domestically and globally.

- Companies need to begin diversifying their employee base to better relate to the emerging marketplace.

# BUSINESS IMPERATIVE #1:

# CHANGING DEMOGRAPHICS

Because we see diversity as an asset, we will attract and fully develop talent from the full range of the world's rich cultural base. It is from this increasingly diverse pool of talent that our future leadership will come.[7]

> -   Public Hearing
>     Testimony to Glass Ceiling Commission
>     Procter & Gamble
>     September 26, 1994

## A WORLD OF DIFFERENCE

When corporations in every industry sector in the U.S. and globally look in the mirror or out in the marketplace, they no longer see mostly white men in blue jackets. They see a world where differences are multiplying as the world shrinks. The typical customer is changing. The composition of the workforce here in America and in the world is changing. As *Business Week* reported, "the marketplace has gone global and isn't going back home again."[8]

## THE GLOBAL POPULATION

If we view the world today as a global village of 100 people with all human ratios remaining the same, the following distribution would occur:

| | |
|---|---:|
| Asia | 57 |
| Europe | 21 |
| Americas/Canada | 14 |
| Africa | 8 |
| Female | 51 |
| Male | 49 |
| Non-white | 70 |
| White | 30 |
| Non-Christian | 70 |
| Christian | 30 |
| Heterosexual | 89 |
| Homosexual | 11 |

Source: Robert L. Dilenschneider, Annual Reports to Clients, 1997

This compressed perspective of our global population frames diversity in an important way. It serves to remind us that the existing and potential players in this global economy are not only from cultures very different from our own, in less fortunate circumstances than many of us, but exist in numbers far greater than we might have realized.

In mid-2000, the world population reached 6.1 billion and is currently growing by 77 million people per year (or 200,000 a day) at a rate of a little over one percent. According to the World Bank, five people are born and two die every second.[9]

The Census Bureau equates the growth in another way. The increase in global population is currently equivalent to adding a new Israel, Egypt, Jordan, West Bank and Gaza to the existing world total each year. The United Nations tracks annual population growth by region. Following are their most recent data:

| Population Estimates | 2000 (millions) | 2001 (millions) | %Change |
|---|---|---|---|
| World Total | 6,057 | 6,145 | 1.3 |
| Africa | 794 | 813 | 2.4 |
| Latin America | 346 | 351 | 1.4 |
| Asia | 3,672 | 3,721 | 1.3 |
| North America | 487 | 493 | 1.2 |
| Europe | 727 | 726 | -0.1 |

Source: United Nations

Regionally, 99% of the growth occurs in the less developed countries in Africa, Asia and Latin America and the Caribbean. In 15 years, Africa has seen a population growth rate of 43.9%; Latin America and the Caribbean, 26.5%; and Asia, 23.6%. These regions include countries that are least able to provide basic health care, education and jobs. Not coincidentally, their life expectancy rates are lower. A child born in sub-Saharan Africa, for example, is far more likely to die in infancy and has a lower life expectancy than a child born anywhere else in the world.[10]

Much of this growth will occur in urban areas. The major urban centers trading today - New York, Tokyo, London - will be joined by Sao Paolo, Jakarta, Delhi, Mexico City and Mumbai, the future centers of commerce and cultural mixing. Like the cities in the developed world, these cities will become the hotbeds of innovation and creativity, expressed in new contexts and in new ways. Because of their sheer size, they will also become important consumer markets.

## POPULATION PROJECTIONS

Over the next few decades, the population of low and middle-income people in developing countries will more than double to *seven billion.* In comparison, population growth in high-income developing countries will increase by only *one billion.*

Europe is experiencing negative growth and the greatest gap in birth and death rates, with more deaths than births occurring annually. In addition to very low birth rates, they have a population of 65 years and older, that is twice the size of the rest of the world, comprising 15% of the total.

By 2050, the global population is projected to reach approximately nine billion. The populations in developing countries are projected to triple in the next fifty years.

### MOST POPULOUS COUNTRIES, 2050

| Countries | Population (in millions) |
|---|---|
| India | 1,572 |
| China | 1,462 |
| U.S. | 397 |
| Pakistan | 344 |
| Indonesia | 311 |
| Nigeria | 279 |
| Bangladesh | 265 |
| Brazil | 247 |
| Congo | 204 |

Source: UN World Population
Prospects: The 2000 Revision

In that same timeframe, it is projected that only three of the developed countries, the U.S., Russia and Japan, will remain as the world's most populous. Only the U.S. will retain its current ranking as third largest; Russia and Japan will fall two places each to tenth and eleventh respectively. Other countries that are expected to be smaller include Italy, Germany and Hungary.

Globally, the number of persons sixty-years-old and older will more than triple. The increase in the number of the eldest old (80 years and above) will

14

increase five-fold, creating a significant elderly support burden on the world community.

International migration is expected to remain high during the 21st century, with the more developed nations continuing to be the net receivers. It is interesting to note that without immigration, the population of the more developed regions would start to decline as a whole within one year, rather than twenty-five.

What does this mean for U.S. businesses? The changing world demographics present unique challenges and significant opportunities for companies that operate in the global economy. The challenges have to do with the increasing diversity of our world village. The opportunities are that these existing and emerging global players are potential business partners, stockholders, customers and employees. As their population and diversity continue to increase, so does their economic growth and power to purchase U.S. goods and services.

## THE U.S. POPULATION

There are dramatic demographic shifts occurring in the U.S. as well. In the last decade the American population grew older and became more racially and ethnically diverse. This change has been felt mostly in the West and South. The U.S. population grew to almost 273 million, an increase of almost 10% since the last census.

How have diverse populations in the U.S. increased? They have traditionally grown in two ways: through natural increase (the excess of births over deaths) and through immigration (immigration minus emigration). Immigration and natural increase have driven growth of Latino and Asian populations. A third source of growth is self-identification. Native Americans, gays and lesbians, people with disabilities and biracial individuals have benefited the most in increases from self-identification.

The 2000 Census provided us with a wake-up call, showing figures that demonstrated just how dramatic and rapid the change has been over the past decade.[11] Rates of growth by the four major racial and ethnic groups were:[12]

```
Asian-Americans . . . . . . . . . . . . . . . . . . . . . . . . . 72.2%
Latinos . . . . . . . . . . . . . . . . . . . . . . . . . . . . . . . . 57.9%
African-Americans . . . . . . . . . . . . . . . . . . . . . . . 21.5%
Whites . . . . . . . . . . . . . . . . . . . . . . . . . . . . . . . . . .8.6%
Overall Population . . . . . . . . . . . . . . . . . . . . . . . 13.2%
```
Source: U.S. Census Bureau

America's changing demographic landscape also reflects rapidly growing Arab and Jewish populations as well as other ethnic constituencies. Significant results of the 2000 census include:

- Latinos have surpassed African-Americans as the largest ethnic group in the U.S.

- Asian-Americans, though still a relatively small percentage of the overall population, grew even more significantly than Latinos over the past decade.

- Life expectancy has increased over the past decade, and the aging population has grown substantially as well.

- Changes in the demographic landscape of the U.S. are impacted by the continuous influx of immigrants, who are typically younger with higher fertility rates and lower education levels than the native-born Americans.

- Immigration has accounted for more than one-third of the growth of the minority population in the past two decades. They comprise approximately 10% of the U.S. population, largely Latino and Asian.[13]

For the first time, participants in the 2000 Census could self-identify as more than one race. Of the 270+ million who participated, 6.8 million, or 2.5%, so identified. Of those, 33% were Latino.

By 2040, the Census Bureau predicts people of color will equal whites, 25% being comprised of Latinos and the other 25% comprised of African-Americans, Asian-Americans and Native Americans. These groups accounted for two-thirds of the growth in U.S. population in the last two decades. [14]

Today, for Americans age 60 years and up, whites outnumber people of color 5:1. For Americans age 10 to 19, that ratio is 2:1. For children under 10, the ratio is 1.5:1, whites to people of color. We are truly becoming a nation of mixed races and multiculturalism.

Some companies are already recognizing the necessity to expand their emphasis on multiculturalism and develop strategies for recruiting diverse workers. A few have recognized the buying power ethnic and multicultural constituencies in the U.S. now possess and are developing marketing strategies to attract these groups, both here in the U.S. and in the emerging markets of our global economy. The influence of multicultural consumers is expanding in every industry. This represents a huge opportunity for Corporate America.

Consider the changes in population this country will see between now and the next fifty years:[15]

|        | 1990 | 2000 | 2050 |
|--------|------|------|------|
| White  | 76%  | 70%  | 53%  |
| Black  | 12%  | 13%  | 14%  |
| Latino | 9%   | 13%  | 25%  |
| Asian  | 3%   | 4%   | 8%   |

Sources: U.S. Census Bureau; The Hudson Institute

In 1990, whites comprised a majority in 70 of the largest cities in the U.S. Today, whites are a majority in 52 of these cities. According to the 2000 Census, ten cities in Texas gained one million Latinos in the last decade. Nationwide, Latino populations more than doubled in 32 cities in the same timeframe. Minorities are now a "majority" in Honolulu, Los Angeles, Miami and San Antonio.

More than half of America's population resides in five states: California, Texas, New York, Florida and Illinois. California now has a "minority majority" population comprised of Latinos, Asian-Americans and African-Americans, who collectively outnumber whites. In 1990, whites comprised 57% of California's population; in 1999, they comprised 49.8%. Hawaii, the second current minority-majority state, has an Asian-American population of 58%.

It is projected that by 2020, New Mexico and Texas will be minority majority states. It should be noted, however, that there are still states with little to no ethnic or racial diversity, such as the northern New England states and West Virginia.

# POPULATION TRENDS

## Latinos

In the past decade, Latinos were the second fastest growing group in the U.S. at almost 60%, nearly five times as fast as the general population. At 35.3 million and 13.2% of the overall population, they outpaced African-Americans to become the largest ethnic group in the U.S. Immigrants contributed significantly to the growth, with Mexican-Americans being the largest sub-group at seven million. Puerto Ricans are the next largest, and Cuban-Americans are third.

The majority of Latinos live in the West and South, 43.5% and 32.8% respectively. Half of all Latinos live in three states, California, Texas and Florida.

Latino-owned businesses have increased by 30% over the past decade to 1.2 million. They employ 1.3 million people and generate $186 billion in revenue. Latino-owned businesses comprise 39.5% of all minority businesses here in the U.S. Cubans have the highest business-ownership rate, more than half of which are in the Miami area.

## Asian-Americans

Over the past decade, Asian-Americans have been the fastest growing group in the U.S. at 72%. They include people from locations as disparate as India, Manchuria and Samoa. They practice different religions, speak different languages and use different alphabets.

With 11.9 million or 3.6% of the U.S. population (the third largest ethnic group), they produce 10% of our engineers. Almost half of all Asian-Americans live in the West, particularly California and Hawaii. Chinese-Americans make up the largest contingency of our Asian population, followed by Filipino-Americans and Asian-Indian-Americans. This latter group has seen a surge in their population in the U.S. through immigration to meet the requirements for Information Technology (IT) professionals. Asian-Indian-Americans are also the wealthiest of all Asian-Americans.

Asian-owned businesses have increased by 30% over the past decade to 913,000, producing record revenues of $307 billion (up 68%) in the same period, compared to a 40% rate for U.S. businesses overall. Much of this success can be attributed to the educational levels attained by this group overall.

They employ 2.2 million. Asian-American businesses comprise 30% of all minority-owned businesses in the U.S., although they make up only 13% of the minority population. The largest percent of businesses are owned by Korean-Americans, followed by Asian-Indian-Americans, Chinese-Americans, Vietnamese-Americans and Japanese-Americans. Hawaiians and Filipino-Americans are much less likely than other Asian sub-groups to own their own businesses.

## African-Americans

The African-American population at 34.7 million, or 12.9% of the overall population, is now the second largest racial/ethnic group in the U.S., increasing by 21.5% over the last decade. This group is growing more slowly than others. Part of this can be explained by the fact that the African-American population lacked the "push" of immigration from Africa and the Caribbean comparable to the number of Latinos immigrating from Latin America.

African-Americans tend to be the most widely dispersed minority population. Over half of all African-Americans live in the South. Slightly less than 20% live in the Midwest, and approximately the same number live in the Northeast. The number of African-Americans living in the nation's largest cities has risen by 6% in the past decade.

African-American-owned businesses increased by 22% to 824,000 in the past decade. They earned $71.2 billion in revenues and employ over 718,000. African-American businesses comprise 27.5% of total minority-owned businesses in the U.S.

## LGBT Community

Historically, the numbers of lesbian, gay, bisexual and transgender (LGBT) people in this country have been underreported given the perceived risks of self-identifying. However, that fear seems to have abated in the past few years, accounting for a significant hike in their demographics. Estimates of gays in this country range from 3% to 10% of the overall population, or between 13 and 17 million people.

Bob Witeck, CEO of Witeck-Combs Communication, which conducts research on gay and lesbian issues, believes the number to be about 15 million, or 6.5% of the overall population. *Gfn.com*, one of the largest and most

19

influential gay websites, agrees, stating that in their research, 15 million gays have self-identified. How much this number increases when "closeted" gays are included is unknown.[16]

## Women

Today, women comprise 52% of the population and 46.6% of the workforce here in the U.S. By 2020 they will be 50 percent. Women-owned businesses have increased 43% in the last decade to approximately eight million firms, generating over $1.4 trillion in sales. Women are forming new businesses at twice the rate as men. Women head up 28% of all (non-farm) businesses in the U.S. They employ 15.5 million people, 35% more than all of the Fortune 500 companies. The University of Michigan has completed research that indicates that companies with women executives who make an initial public offering (IPO) are valued higher than newly public companies with an all male management team.[17]

In Corporate America women have moved up the ranks relatively slowly. According to the Catalyst organization, while women hold almost half the lower and mid-level managerial positions at Fortune 500 companies, they occupy only 7% to 9% of senior leadership positions. In 1996, women occupied 10% of all officer positions in companies; in 2000, those ranks had increased by only 2.5%. There is still a pay disparity between men and women, with men earning one and a half times overall more than women. It is not surprising that women are leaving the corporate sector at twice the rate of men.

## Aging Americans

Age (65 and over) contributes the most significant change in U.S. demographics. Boomers are aging. Just as they strained the capacity of elementary schools in the 1950s, the capacity of elder care facilities are being pressed today. The population of older Americans will increase while the population of younger Americans, age 16 to 24, will continue to decrease. By 2020, 20% of the population will be 65 or older, matching the percentage of 20 to 35 year-olds. By 2050 the aging population will double with more 85+ year-olds than ever before. This is due in large part to the low birth rate amongst baby boomers and to the fact that longevity has increased dramatically over the past decade. For the first time in our history, there are more elderly persons then teenagers.

The health of aging Americans has improved greatly. They are living longer and will be working longer, deferring retirement. Within two years, workers age 55 and older are expected to grow by 43%. In fact, many who reach age 65 will continue to require outside income, being unable to retire. This is even truer today, given current poor economic conditions that decrease the value of 401K plans and increase rampant restructuring that often impacts the aging worker.

In the next several decades, it is predicted that retirement, as we know it today, will disappear. Seniors will continue to have more leisure time. Already well-educated, this group will be interested in continuing lifelong learning through traditional educational institutions, thereby helping to fill an anticipated shortage of students matriculating at colleges and universities due to a lower birth rate.

Improved medicine and genetic engineering will likely contribute to even greater longevity. However, as the older population ages, health care needs are likely to increase. Longevity may still mean several years of life spent with some chronic disease or disability. A declining workforce will challenge the ability of the health care industry to provide services for the elderly at a time when needs are increasing.

## Native Americans

With a population of 4.1 million, Native Americans grew 255% in the last three decades. This increase reflects a tendency among Americans of partial Indian ancestry to reclaim heritage. Contrary to popular belief, most in this group live in major cities, not on reservations. There are more than 500 recognized tribes, but half of all Native Americans belong to one of eight of the major tribes: the largest of which are Cherokee, Navajo, Chippewa, and Sioux.

Native Americans own approximately 200,000 businesses in the U.S., which represents 3% of the total minority-owned businesses. They employ 300,000 and generated revenues of $34.3 billion, an increase of 84%, compared to an average 7% increase for all small businesses. Most of their businesses are in the service sector. The number of Native American businesses grew 12 times faster than all U.S. firms.

One third of all businesses owned by Native Americans are in four states: California, Texas, Oklahoma and Florida. Not surprisingly, this data correlates with the fact that three of every ten Native Americans reside in these states. Alaska has the highest proportion of businesses with 11%.

## People with Disabilities

Like gays and lesbians, obtaining accurate numbers on this group is a challenge, because, they, too, must self-identify. It is estimated that there are 54 million disabled, or approximately 20% of the U.S. population, of all backgrounds, cultures and ages. This is a larger sub-group than either Latinos or African-Americans. The number of people with disabilities has increased by 25% in the last decade, part of which can be attributed to a greater willingness to self-identify. As the population ages, the likelihood of acquiring a disability increases.

Very few families are left untouched by a person with a disability. Of 70 million families in the U.S., 20 million have at least one member with a disability. Disability rates amongst families are 32% for African-Americans, 29% for whites, 23% for Latinos and 22% for other races and ethnicities.

Forty percent of the disabled population have on-line access, twice the number of non-disabled people. This is significant when one considers that some disabilities prevent the use of a computer and that all disabled people do not have assistive technology to facilitate this process.

Globally, it is estimated that there are over 500 million people with disabilities. For countries that track data on people with disabilities, the approximate ratios are as follows:

> 1 in 5 . . . . . . . . . . . . . . . . . . U.S.
> 1 in 6 . . . . . . . . . . . . . . . . . . Australia
> 1 in 7 . . . . . . . . . . . . . . . . . . Canada
> 1 in 10 . . . . . . . . . . . . . . . . Europe

(Variables such as integrity of tracking methodology and level of comfort with self-identification can affect data.)

## Next Generation Americans

Even though the population of teen-agers is decreasing in the U, S., there are still 31.6 million of this group, defined as between the ages of 12 and 19. The percentage of people of color that comprise this group is increasing. Today, the ratio is two whites to one person of color in this age group. By 2040, or sooner, it is projected to become equal. Already, Latino teens comprise the minority majority in urban areas such as Miami, San Antonio and East Los Angeles.

## CHALLENGES AND OPPORTUNITIES

Globally, the demographic changes have been significant. Regions with the most growth include Africa, Latin America and Asia. These expanding emerging markets are predominantly populated by people of ethnic and racial diversity. In order to develop true cultural synergy and effective partnerships with these global markets - not to mention design and sell product to them, businesses in the U.S. need to establish a new priority:

> *to acquire global intelligence about the cultures with which they will be doing business, particularly in the emerging markets.*

Individuals within these groups are beginning to reflect a much broader range of interests and consumer needs.

Clearly, if businesses are to succeed in the coming decades, they need to be able to attract an increasingly diverse workforce, domestically and globally. To do so, companies need to ensure their corporate cultures are regarded as inclusive and welcoming to people of difference. Businesses also need to continually expand their customer base. In addition to a quality product delivered on time, customers are looking for companies that design product to meet their specific needs (often influenced by their diversity) and marketed with their differences in mind. Of course, this has to be followed up with great customer service delivered by a team that can relate well to consumer diversity and that understands the nuances of different cultures.

## CONCLUSION

Why are these demographic changes important? Understanding demographic trends helps businesses identify which markets are likely to fragment into targets that are appropriate to their products and services. These smaller demographic groups will drive future market growth, demanding new products and services to meet their unique needs and preferences.

In the U.S. people of color will increasingly shape the national character, adding racial and ethnic diversity to schools, workplaces and governments. A multicultural America has a competitive advantage in the global economy. The U.S. is geographically positioned to serve the growing Asian and Latin American markets. America's increasingly multicultural population can enhance its ability to succeed in the new global marketplace. With ties to all regions and diversities of the world, people of color in the U.S. can help our businesses understand the needs and preferences of people in other countries.

# SUMMARY HIGHLIGHTS
# Business Imperative 1: Changing Demographics

- 99 % of the world population growth occurs in Africa, Asia and Latin America.

- These existing and emerging global players are potential business partners, stockholders, customers and employees. As their population and diversity continue to increase, so does their economic growth and power to purchase U.S. goods and services.

- The 2000 Census is a wake-up call demonstrating how dramatic and rapid the change in U.S. demographics has been in the last decade.

- Latinos have surpassed African-Americans as the largest ethnic group in the U.S.

- Minority and women-owned businesses have increased significantly in the U.S:

| Multicultural Group | # Businesses | #Employed | Revenues |
|---|---|---|---|
| Women | 8 million | 15.5 million | $1.4 trillion |
| Latinos | 1.2 million | 1.3 million | $186 billion |
| Asian-Americans | 918,000 | 2.2 million | $307 billion |
| African-Americans | 824,000 | 718,000 | $ 71 billion |
| Native Americans | 200,000 | 300,000 | $ 34 billion |

- For the first time in our history, there are more elderly persons than teenagers.

- Understanding demographic trends helps businesses identify which markets are likely targets for their products.

25

# BUSINESS IMPERATIVE #2:

# EXPANDING GLOBAL ECONOMY

Being global means that our customers are diverse. Our stockholders are diverse. The population which is available to us, our productivity, creativity, innovation and people who supply us are diverse. There is no way we can run a business effectively without a deep understanding and accommodation of these elements.

> - Charles L. Reid III, Past Director
>   Diversity[18]
>   Kraft General Foods

## THE NEW BUSINESS UNIT

The world is the new business unit, and the economic and social forces that shape the marketplace are global. Over the past decade the global economy has been experiencing exponential growth. The world is the new business unit, not only as a marketplace but as a source of jobs and new technology as well. Wealth creation is now dependent on a world economy. Conditions have changed in support of diversity.

World markets intersect daily. Business consolidations are occurring on a global level. Companies acquiring or merging with other companies half way around the world are a daily occurrence. More than ever before, corporations need diverse people and their skills to facilitate such strategic consolidations and mergers. Not surprisingly, 60% of the mergers, acquisitions and joint ventures that occur today are unsuccessful due to poor planning and the failure to address the issue of cultural compatibility. According to a Society of Human Resources Management (SHRM) study, globalization is cited as the most critical issue facing HR leaders in the next decade.

A new landscape is emerging across the business world. The old boundaries of national economies and markets are giving way to globalization, much like the crumbling of traditional office walls and hierarchical corporate structures and the disappearance of such concepts as "lifelong employment." The economic exchange across borders of goods, services and labor, which are key indicators of economic growth, is increasing. Global competition may eventually lead to the demise of domestic territorialism.

The Chairman and CEO of Work in America Institute, Inc., Jerome M. Roscow, elaborates that in a global economy:

> Competition transcends national boundaries, driven by increasingly sophisticated channels of communication, the instantaneous transmittal of information on a worldwide basis, and by new and faster methods of capital transfer.[19]

Expanding emerging markets are dominated by developing and underdeveloped countries, which are predominantly populated by people of diverse ethnic and racial backgrounds. These regions include the Pacific Rim, Eastern Asia, Eastern and Central Europe and Mexico and South and Central America.

## FACTORS PROMOTING THE GLOBAL ECONOMY

World trade leads to economic growth. A country that opens itself up to world trade benefits from an increased growth rate and a higher GDP.

As other nations, particularly those emerging in the global economy, begin competing with the U.S. labor force for lower skilled jobs and lower wages, the result is that this level of work will continue to disappear from the American landscape. Displaced U.S. workers will have to be reskilled. The positive ramification of this trend somewhat offsets the negative. Workers in these emerging countries will now be able to afford more American exported goods and services. As a result, markets for U.S. products, services and capital will become broader and deeper. As *Workforce 2020* reminds us:

> Globalization is good for America because it allows us to specialize in producing those goods and services in which we have the greatest comparative advantage. By enabling us to use our labor and other resources in industries and occupations in which our productivity is highest and growing rapidly, globalization helps raise incomes and living standards in America.[20]

Another trend promoting the global economy has been tremendous technological breakthroughs, such as the Internet and wireless communication. Because of these technologies, distance poses fewer obstacles and time constraints. Technology will continue to dissolve boundaries, which will increase globalization, driving what Theodore Levitt calls the "converging commonality." This is boosted by global transportation and communication costs, which have plummeted to lower rates.

There are some sociological benefits to underdeveloped nations that participation in the global economy offers. Economic growth contributes to the reduction of poverty. While the benefits of globalization have most positively impacted poverty levels in the two fastest growing regions of the world, East Asia and Pacific & South Asia, all developing countries can benefit once economic growth is achieved and can be sustained.

Developing nations are beginning to recognize that deregulation and liberalization of business ownership, capital investment and trade agreements are key to rapid growth and are more aggressively supporting these changes as a result.

## THE DIGITAL DIVIDE

The potential that globalization will bring to emerging markets also illuminates the wide disparity that exists between the "haves" and the "have-nots." Technology provides powerful solutions to ameliorating the disparity, enabling developing countries to focus on creating wealth, reducing poverty levels and raising standards of living. Technology assists people in connecting with others worldwide, whom they may not know, but with whom they share similar interests, passions and lifestyles. The bottom line for Corporate America is that these countries will dramatically increase their ability to purchase goods and services as a result.

At a recent National Association of Broadcasters conference that convened CEOs from digital companies and other experts, many possibilities for eradicating the gap that exists globally between the "haves" and the "have-nots" through the use of digital technologies and the Internet, were revealed. As Colin Powell stated in his introductory remarks, "if digital apartheid persists, we all lose. The digital have-nots will be poorer, more resentful of progress than ever ..." and will not be able to become the skilled workers and potential customers that are needed to sustain the growth of the new economy. Following are some of the more stimulating observations by several key presenters at the conference:

- "The Internet's openness to communication is profound." This describes the impact of broadcasting globally over the Net in 50 different languages from 90 different countries. (Rob Glaser, CEO, RealNetworks)

- "The developing world may have the opportunity to skip entire layers of infrastructure...telephone poles with all the copper wire... billions of dollars on malls...that could save a tremendous amount of energy, building materials, time and money." (Jeff Bezos, CEO, Amazon.com)

- The global transformation now underway, a "digital renaissance," promotes the tools for invention that can be extended to every corner of the earth. A new H-P division, World e-Inclusion, plans to sell, lease or donate $1 billion in products and services to developing countries, which H-P believes will create "digital dividends" - profits, social benefits and novel business opportunities. (Carly Fiorina, CEO, Hewlitt-Packard)

- There is a market opportunity serving the "bottom of the economic pyramid," namely the four billion people with incomes less than $1,500 a year. "Don't look at the poor and say there is no hope. Selling to the poor may be more profitable than selling to you and me. This is where the future is. This digital divide is not about lack of opportunity; it is about lack of imagination." (C.K. Prahalad, University of Michigan business professor)

- The power of entrepreneurial energy drives beneficial change: an historic partnership between the "increasingly talent-constrained but capital-rich industrial world" and "the capital-starved developing regions with their huge pools of underutilized human talent..."(Vinod Khosla, venture capitalist)[21]

## ESTABLISHING HUMAN CONNECTIVITY

Given the forces in place that are continuing to propel us to increased global interdependence, how can companies hone their skills in order to optimize their participation in this new global business unit? The answer is through acquiring global intelligence and cultural competence.

### Global Intelligence

With increasing market competition both in the U. S. and abroad, it is imperative that businesses develop skills in understanding and relating to a large spectrum of cultures, ethnicities and lifestyles. Further, they must formalize and institutionalize this process throughout their businesses. Acquiring global intelligence requires that intercultural learning occur through a series of continual encounters with new cultural situations. This capability will provide companies with competitive advantage, the fodder by which innovative products and services are created, marketed and sold to customers globally.

Leveraging global intelligence can sustain demand for product, resulting in profits that send competitors back to the drawing board. General Motors, for example, has established a global Center of Expertise on Diversity and

Growth Markets, which can tap into the cultural nuances of consumers globally and provide insight to their current demands.

Our new global business unit requires a new mindset, one of inclusion and collaboration. Acquiring global intelligence will not only help a business succeed, it will foster a new sense of community.

## The Components of Cultural Competence

To many in Corporate America, acquiring cultural competence means learning about the customs and mores in various countries in which their respective companies conduct business. I refer to this as the "quick study" approach, where information about protocol, customs and etiquette of a particular country is communicated in a short segment of time.

This exercise usually precedes travel to that particular region of the world in order to optimize the traveler's ability to conduct business successfully while there. Such topics as hand gestures, body language, tipping, gift giving and receiving, greetings, punctuality, conversational no-nos are usually covered in this type of training - all extremely useful information, to be sure, but limited and somewhat superficial, nevertheless.

There is, however, another perspective - one that is essential in defining the complexities of cultural diversity and one that will more effectively promote success for companies over the long-term. This deeper, more comprehensive approach to acquiring cultural competence is presented in the fascinating book by O'Hara-Devereaux and Johansen entitled, *GlobalWork: Bridging Distance, Culture & Time.*

They identify changes that are of such magnitude, that they have caused ripple effects globally. These changes, or "fault lines," include:

• The globalization of consumerism.

• The transformation of the traditional corporate hierarchy into a global, multinational network.

• The fragmentation of work and resulting creation of global jobs.

• The ascendancy of knowledge as a global product.

The authors note that, in order to make globalwork real and successful, where "workspace" replaces workplace, an appreciation of these changes and how to effectively respond to them is vital in creating a major paradigm shift in how companies will do business. This transformation presents some challenging questions:

- What are the new rules of work?

- Given the multinational, multicultural participants in global work, what are the new ethics?

- Where are the new boundaries?

This radical transformation, the authors suggest, will prompt corporations to create a globally shared vision based on a new "third way" culture. (A "third way" culture is one that combines the best practices of all cultures, rather than one dominating or absorbing another.) This emerging global culture is one that ascribes wealth to collective wisdom and power to information workers, in effect leveling the playing field for participants. According to O'Hara-Devereaux and Johansen, these workers will prevail in the global economy of the future. [22]

The complexities of multiculturalism are addressed through a model comprised of five cultural lenses identified by the authors. This model provides a framework and focus for businesses operating in a global economy to acquire a firm understanding of the key macro-level questions that need to be addressed in creating successful organizations. These questions include:

- What are the cultural influences in this situation?

- How can they be understood so that an inclusive, people-oriented climate is maintained and productivity and creativity enhanced?

The five cultural lenses that comprise the model include:[23]

1. **Language:** Fluency in several languages enables a greater array of relationships and business advantages. Americans' insistence on English has created some bitterness and serious communication issues with would-be business partners. Facility with several languages will be a needed competency in the future for any player in the global economy.

2. **Context:** Americans tend to be low-context, (a strong reliance on detailed, objective information, the access to which is highly controlled). Low-context cultures also tend to be more task-oriented. Meetings and agendas are planned well in advance. Competence is given more weight than title or status. Rewards are bestowed for individual performance. Competitiveness and assertiveness are encouraged by the culture.

   Asians, on the other hand, tend to be high-context, where there is less expectation for detailed information and where information, which is largely subjective, is shared. Meetings are often called on short notice with no particular agenda. High-context cultures tend to be more relationship-oriented, where authority and status, as opposed to merit, are ascribed importance. Rewards are group-oriented. Humility and face-saving are encouraged in these cultures.

3. **Time:** Americans tend to worship time and manage it as though it were a scarce resource. In many countries, time is treated more flexibly. Being late, as in some Latin American cultures, may be the norm. Americans tend to be oriented to the present, influenced by the short-term future, always believing that they have control over the present and future. Asian cultures tend to be oriented toward a more distant future. Latin cultures are more past-oriented; believing that the past controls the present and future.

4. **Power Equality:** Cultures in Asian and Latin countries tend to ascribe power and equality based on predetermined conditions such as social class, age, wealth, education, race and family. The U.S. and northern Europe, on the other hand, believe that power is earned and tend to bristle at the uneven application of rules and existing inequalities. Power equality, more than any other cultural variable, is the most challenging to a multinational, multicultural business operating in the global economy whose structure is likely to be flat and decentralized.

5. **Information Flow**: Information flows freely in high context cultures that rely on interpersonal contacts and a sea of information, such as in Latin America. A constant bombardment of information creates a fast flow rate. Low context cultures, such as the U.S., control and compartmentalize information, allowing access only to screened people with a "need to know." The flow of information tends to be much slower.

## CHALLENGES & OPPORTUNITIES

O'Hara-Devereaux and Johansen note that globalization impacts not only the economy, but how we do our work. The concept, "globalwork," refers to increasing challenges as well as opportunities for businesses to interact and collaborate on a global basis. The key is recognizing the importance of culture in globalwork.

Some of these challenges include identifying business systems that will be impacted by very different cultures. For example, performance evaluations will be challenging when members of high and low-context cultures work together. When the phrase, "right away," can mean - depending on the culture - instantly, in an hour, in a day, in a few weeks, expectations about time and rules that will be acceptable to a mix of cultures will need to be defined. Clearly, the challenge for global corporations to manage a balance of information flow between "enough" and "overload" will be important to satisfy the needs of participating cultures.

Until new models of global corporate culture are revised and implemented, workers will continue to operate under the old value and belief system, thereby creating obstacles to the globalization of corporations. Clearly, new competencies in leadership and teamwork need defining. In the end, globalwork will require flexibility and adaptation of all cultural perspectives, where no one will have the comfort of being totally "at home" or "in balance."

The opportunity for corporations and the multicultural individuals involved in establishing "globalwork" will be the potential for significant organizational and personal growth. A positive to acquiring global intelligence and cultural competence is that we will be more aware of our own cultural heritage.

> The irony is that until we undertake the hard work of cross-cultural learning, we cannot really understand much about ourselves. For the beginning of self-knowledge lies in seeing ourselves reflected in the cultural prism of others. We learn the strengths and the weaknesses of our own cultural myths and mores...Until we really understand ourselves, we cannot begin to understand others.[24]

If companies are up to the task of performing due diligence in acquiring global intelligence and collaborating on a multicultural level that this new global business unit will require, their reward will be increased opportunities to expand their customer base and increase profitability.

## CONCLUSION

Globalization is opening up tremendous opportunities for profitable business relationships, cooperative ventures and collective growth. A company's ability to understand and serve its diverse customer base well is directly related to its ability to foster diversity within its own ranks. After all, how does a business practice multiculturalism externally in an authentic way if it cannot do so internally amongst its own ranks? Cultural diversity must not be viewed by business leaders just as a new rule of engagement in the global economy, but as an *advantage* that will positively impact their bottom line.

## SUMMARY HIGHLIGHTS
# Business Imperative 2: Expanding Global Economy

- The world is the new business unit, not only as a marketplace but as a source of jobs and new technology.

- Wealth creation is now dependent on a world economy. Conditions have changed in support of diversity.

- More than ever before, corporations need diverse people and their skills to facilitate consolidations and mergers.

- According to a SHRM study, globalization is cited as the most critical issue facing HR leaders in the next decade.

- The old boundaries of national economies and markets are giving way to globalization.

- A country that opens itself up to world trade benefits from an increased growth rate, higher GDP and decreased poverty levels.

- Lower-skilled jobs are being outsourced to emerging countries with lower cost structures. U.S. workers will be displaced by global workers and will have to be reskilled.

- Workers in the emerging countries will be able to afford more U.S. goods and services.

- Businesses must practice acquiring global intelligence and developing cultural competence to optimize their participation in the global economy.

- Acquiring global intelligence will not only help a business succeed, it will foster a new sense of community.

- To be successful, companies will need to transform how they do business in the global economy, adopting a "global" culture that includes best practices from all cultures.

- Cultural diversity must be viewed as more than just a new rule of engagement in the global economy.  It must be viewed as an **advantage** that will positively impact the bottom line.

.

# BUSINESS IMPERATIVE #3:

## EMERGING CUSTOMER BASE

The market place is the driving force behind everything
we do. But the marketplace is not just white males. The
population of minorities in this country totals some 84
million, more than the entire population of Germany,
but look at the amount of attention paid to them vs. foreign countries.

-   Rai Cockfield, Vice-President,
    Market Development
    IBM[25]

## CUSTOMERS

Our customers are changing. As the percentage of diversity increases in the overall population both here and abroad, so does the diversity of customers. Emerging markets, the increasingly lucrative global ethnic markets, represent one of the largest growth sectors in the years to come.

If a company is to increase its penetration in these markets and expand market share, its workforce must understand the unique needs of people from different cultures and regions, either by having lived there or, at the very least, traveled there. Sales will be marginalized if a company doesn't have employees in product development and design that understand the requirements of these diverse markets.

Globalization and competitive advantage demand that companies build a diverse workforce and train them to be culturally competent and that it be done faster than the competitors'. A company's growth needs to leverage its gains in growing diverse markets.

## PURCHASING POWER OF GLOBAL DIVERSE MARKETS

While the majority of global middle-class consumers continue to reside in North America, Japan and Western Europe, the growth of this market over the next two decades will be greatest in Eastern Europe, Asia (excluding Japan) and Latin America. These emerging middle class consumers currently comprise 18% but are expected to increase their share to one-third by 2010. This equates to a 5% growth rate for the emerging markets compared to a 2% growth rate for the industrialized nations.

In less than ten years these three emerging regions will represent a consumer market that is the size of Europe and the U.S. today. Clearly, the most stunning economic growth will continue to be in Asia, where, (excluding Japan and China; which alone experiences a growth of 10%) the average growth rate for the past decade has been a phenomenal 7%. The consumer market in Latin America should also expand exponentially, at least doubling in size in every country. The most obvious result of this incredible income growth is an explosive demand for consumer products.

The World Bank has traditionally used the Gross National Product (GNP) as an indicator of a country's purchasing health. Recently, it has developed an index called the Purchasing Power Parity (PPP), which is a country's gross national income converted to "international dollars" using a purchasing power parity conversion factor.[26] Simply stated, it is an indicator of a nation's per capita purchasing power of U.S. goods. When the Producer Price Index (PPI) is applied, the value to a U.S. company of including global players in its customer base becomes even more compelling. Randomly selected by region, the following is a sample of global consumers from both developed and developing countries:

## GROSS NATIONAL INCOME IN PURCHASING POWER PARITY PER CAPITA

| Country | (US$) |
|---|---|
| **Europe** | |
| Germany | 22,700 |
| Spain | 17,300 |
| Hungary | 7,800 |
| Poland | 7,200 |
| Russia | 4,200 |
| **Asia** | |
| Singapore | 27,800 |
| Japan | 23,400 |
| Taiwan | 16,100 |
| South Korea | 13,300 |
| China | 3,800 |
| **Africa** | |
| South Africa | 6,900 |
| Botswana | 3,900 |
| Egypt | 3,000 |
| Zimbabwe | 2,400 |
| Ghana | 1,900 |

### Latin America

| | |
|---|---|
| Chile | 12,400 |
| Argentina | 10,000 |
| Mexico | 8,500 |
| Venezuela | 8,000 |
| Brazil | 6,150 |

Source: World Bank

## CUSTOMER DEMANDS

Most readers are aware of the gains women have made as business owners in the U.S., discussed later in this chapter. What is not as well known is the extent of women-owned businesses elsewhere in the world. For example, women own 33% of all businesses in Australia and Canada; 32% in Germany; 24% in Italy and Brazil; 20% in Ireland and 16% in France. Women need to be taken seriously as a major player in the emerging global markets.

Companies who wish to avoid blunders should ensure customer service teams reflect the diversity of the targeted customer's culture in the planning and design phase of a marketing campaign. Major blunders can be avoided when a diverse product development team with a broad range of experiences and thorough understanding of the culture being targeted can more easily question and identify product features and advertising elements that may potentially offend that customer base. Diversity also needs to be represented at the later stage of a product's cycle – on the teams doing the designing and packaging, not to mention sales and customer service.

For many – customer, contractor, supplier, alliance partner, shareholder or potential employee, the diversity of a company's workforce is often one of the critical items on their "checklist" to determine whether or not there will be a future business relationship. Yet, *Fortune* reported in 2002 that executives, especially those who are not diverse, continue to be relatively unaware of the potential purchasing power of ethnic markets.[27]

If representation of its customer base is not reflected in its workforce, a company, at the very least, needs to be diligent in training its employees in global intelligence, the culture and language of existing and *future* customers. Customers tend to trust and respond best to a company with representation of "people like them" on their customer service team. Populating teams with the diversity of emerging markets, enabling them to relate to and think like the customer as well as better understand and predict how products and advertising will play out in those cultures, is a smart business decision. As Theodore Levitt states, personalizing the business relationship in an "obsessively intimate fashion" creates success. If customers don't feel respected and listened to, they will take their business elsewhere. Losing a customer is expensive. It is estimated that it costs companies six times more to acquire a new customer than to retain the current one.

Diversity can create customer understanding and compatibility, helping to keep that customer buying goods and services. One note of caution. Diverse members of customer teams must be viewed and respected as valuable contributors. No one wants to feel exploited for his/her differences.

## PURCHASING POWER OF U.S. DIVERSE MARKETS

The populations of people of color here in the U.S. are growing at a faster pace than that of whites. So is their economic clout. Another way to look at markets is to compare gross domestic product. If the spending power of ethnic Americans were represented separately, it would be the sixth largest market in the world: [28]

### GROSS DOMESTIC PRODUCT

| Market | ($Billions) |
|---|---|
| U.S. | 9,225 |
| China | 4,800[29] |
| Japan | 2,955 |
| Germany | 1,864 |
| India | 1,805 |
| France | 1,373 |
| *Ethnic America* | *1,300* |
| United Kingdom | 1,290 |
| Italy | 1,212 |
| Brazil | 1,057 |
| Mexico | 865 |

Sources: The World Almanac & Book of Facts, 2002 & Selig Center for Economic Growth

U.S. buying power is currently in excess of $9 trillion; people of color alone contribute 14% of that figure, over one trillion a year. According to the Population Reference Bureau, African-Americans, Latinos and Asian-Americans made up 25% of the U.S. consumer base in 2000. The U.S. diversity marketplace now exceeds the Gross Domestic Product (GDP) of the United Kingdom. It is higher in purchasing power than all but four of our leading global trading partners. The total purchasing power for these groups cuts across all industries.

According to the Selig Center for Economic Growth, minority purchasing power has nearly doubled since 1990 and is growing 65% faster than U.S. purchasing power overall. The combined purchasing power of African-Americans, Asian-Americans and Native-Americans will total $1.4 trillion by 2007, more than tripling levels in 1990. A Minority Business Development Agency report is in accordance, noting that minority purchasing power is headed upward to $2 trillion by 2015 and $3 trillion by 2030. In the past decade Asian-American buying power surged 125%, compared to 118% for Latinos and 85% for African-Americans. By contrast, purchasing power amongst whites for the same timeframe increased by 64%. According to the Selig Center for Economic Growth, by 2007 Latino purchasing power will increase 315%, Asian-Americans 287% and African-Americans 170%. [30]

The disposable income of aging Americans, gays and lesbians and people with disabilities combined equates to another $1.6 trillion in diverse purchasing power.[31]

Companies that want competitive advantage not only must understand the constituencies that comprise the multicultural U.S. market, they must aggressively court them. As the U.S. consumer market becomes more diverse, advertising and product development must be tailored to each market segment.

## Factors Positively Impacting Purchasing Power

The economic forces supporting continued growth of purchasing power for the American ethnic and racial populations include:

- Improved employment opportunities.

- Educational gains.

- The number of business start-ups and expansions.

- The demographic trends favoring people of color over whites.

## PURCHASING POWER

### African-Americans

The largest purchasing power of the multiethnic American market belongs to African-Americans. According to the Selig Center for Economic Growth, African-American buying power increased to $646 billion, a compound annual growth rate of six percent. In the next five years, African-Americans are expected to increase their spending by 49%, to almost $853 billion. It is projected that in another ten years, 60% of African-Americans will be middle-class.[32]

Almost four million African-Americans currently have achieved "middle-class" status with an income of $50,000 or more. Over a third of these are considered upper income, with incomes of $75,000 or more. Buying power of middle-class African-Americans alone is expected to increase by almost one-third over the next five years to top $292 billion/year by 2006. Instead of assimilating into white suburbs, middle-class and affluent African-Americans are remaining in cities, comprising at least 40% of the population.

Last year African-Americans spent over $5 billion on consumer electronics, 30% more than the previous year, at twice the rate of white consumers. Since there are 14% more African-American women than men, they hold much of the consumer power for this group.

Forty-four percent have access to the Internet, an increase of over 40% in the last four years. African-Americans are also spending more on telephone services (wireless and traditional), personal care products, children's apparel, footwear, electricity and natural gas.

The three states that have a large percentage of African-American markets as well as the highest rate of growth of purchasing power amongst this constituency group are New York, California and Texas. The share of buying power will rise in every state except California and the District of Columbia, where it is already very high.

## Latinos

The immense buying power of the largest ethnic group in America will energize the U.S. economy as never before. Latino purchasing power grew at a compound annual rate of 7.3% to $581 billion in two years. It is projected to grow faster than African-American or Native American buying power, but not as fast as Asian. By 2007 Latinos are projected to have over $927 billion in disposable income, an increase of 60%.

Growth rates are significantly impacted by both a natural increase in the Latino population as well as immigration. While the share of buying power by Latinos will increase in every state, the top three states with largest share are New Mexico, California and Texas.

Latinos spend more on food, apparel (men's, boy's and children's), household furnishings, footwear and telephone services than any other consumer. Their computer purchases and use of the Internet are also up, (42% of households have computers.)

From a targeted marketing perspective, it is noteworthy that 55% use the Internet in Spanish, 74% watch Spanish television and 60% listen to Spanish radio.

## Asian-Americans

The purchasing power of Asian-Americans increased to $296 billion in the past decade, a huge amount given that this group comprises only 4% of the overall population. Over the next five years, their purchasing power will increase to $455 billion, a 54% increase.

Asian-Americans have the highest median income of any group, ($47,000/year). Of all the subgroups in this category, Asian-Indians have the highest educational levels and are the most affluent, with a median income of $170,000/year. However, companies have rarely targeted this group in the past, bypassing a major marketing opportunity.

The most important forces supporting continued growth in Asian purchasing power include a higher level of education than the average American, an increasing number of Asian-owned businesses and a population that is growing more rapidly than the total population, due to strong immigration.

The states with the largest share of Asian purchasing power include Hawaii (58% Asian), California, New York and New Jersey. The share of buying power is expected to grow in every state except Hawaii, where it is already high.

Many of the purchases of this group include big-ticket items, such as homes, furniture and electronic equipment. Of all multicultural groups, Asian-Americans are most likely to purchase a luxury car. 70% of Asian-Americans are on-line. Telecom companies have successfully targeted this market for several years now, with substantial revenues generated by international calls to Asia.

Asian-Americans remain a largely untapped market. Like Latinos, this may be due in part to the number of cultures under the Asian and Latino umbrellas respectively, as well as the challenge that numerous languages pose.

## Native Americans

While Native Americans comprise less than one percent of the U.S. population, they control almost $41 billion in disposable income, up 95% in the past decade. This number exceeds the growth in buying power for whites (67.4%) and the U.S. population as a whole (70.4%). Though markets in most states are small, given the overall population of Native Americans; they are flourishing, with the largest shares going to California, Oklahoma and Texas. Native Americans are isolated from the rest of America by tribal sovereignty laws. This has enabled some tribes to establish lucrative gambling operations, though only 8% of Native Americans, in fact, gain from casino revenues.

## LGBT Community

Gathering demographics for this group of consumers is difficult because it requires self-identification. Unlike people with disabilities and people of color, who are also asked to self-identify, gays and lesbians feel more threatened by the process. Therefore, it's impossible to know their demographics with any degree of certainty. However, over time, the gay community has begun to view the environment as more tolerant, with companies seeing an increase in the number of gay employee resource groups in their ranks. Estimates are that the purchasing power (the "pink dollar") of this group is currently $514 billion. *Gfn.com*, the largest website for gays, estimates an even higher asset base of between $800 billion and $1 trillion.[33]

A new report on gay spending power conducted by GSociety, a gay marketing group, found that the average combined income for gay couples was 60% higher than the average U.S. income. Another study done by a marketing research firm in San Francisco, Community Marketing Inc., indicated that gays and lesbians are more likely to take a vacation (85%) than their heterosexual counterparts (64%). One of the reasons that this group has a greater willingness to spend money on high-dollar, luxury items than their counterparts may be due to the smaller number of children in gay households. It is also due, however, to considerable discretionary income.

While brand loyalty amongst ethnic Americans is fairly low, it is extremely high amongst gays. They make purchasing decisions based on a company's gay-friendly policies, with 80% of gays more likely to buy product if the company has a gay-friendly policy. Brand loyalty is one of the reasons why ten companies pulled ads from the Dr. Laura radio show, after she made disparaging comments about the gay community. A company would do well to attract such loyalty.

More than any other group, gays purchase goods off of the Internet. Gays spend more time on the Internet (average 21 hours/week) than heterosexuals, and also tend to purchase more goods online than heterosexuals, 63% to 59% respectively.

Gays are more likely to purchase electronic equipment, CDs, books, home improvements, furniture and appliances than heterosexuals. They are twice as likely as heterosexuals to purchase vacation homes, six times more likely to purchase home theater systems and eight times more likely to purchase laptop computers.

## Women

Women now comprise 52% of the population, and more companies are developing marketing strategies that incorporate their buying habits. In the U.S. women now control 85% of consumer spending. American women are the strongest economic force on the planet; they control $5.2 trillion. They purchase between 50 and 82% of all consumer goods, including computers, cars, pharmaceuticals and stocks, of which they now own more than half. Single women, with a combined income of approximately $200 billion, account for a large percentage of apparel and electronic equipment purchases. Women now equal men as users of the Internet.

The number of women having babies later in life has grown 19% in the last decade. In the past five years, women-owned businesses increased by 14% nationwide (twice the rate of all firms), sales increased by 40% and employment grew by 30%. According to research done in 2002 by *Business Week* and *Gallup*, women will soon control 60% of the country's wealth.[34] Women business owners are more likely to make personal purchases on-line compared to other working women, 57% to 40%.

The largest share of women-owned firms is in the service sector. However, women are diversifying into non-traditional sectors with the largest growth in construction, agriculture, transportation, communications and public utilities. The three states with the most women-owned firms are California, Texas and Florida.

This year, there are an estimated 1.2 million firms (15%) owned by women of color, an increase of 32% in the past five years. While women in general have seen an improvement in their access to capital, women of color continue to experience more difficulties than their white counterparts. Overall, women-owned businesses are just as financially strong and creditworthy as men's.

Companies owned by women tend to have greater gender equity and family-friendly policies and a high level of volunteerism and philanthropy.

## Aging Population

Older Americans spend $900 billion annually. The economic status of older people has improved greatly over the past few decades. Poverty levels have declined by almost 25% in the last 40 years. There has been a substantial increase in net worth for many older Americans with increased power to purchase more goods and services that people choose later in life. In fact, older Americans control more than 50% of all discretionary income.

The median net worth of households headed by older persons increased by 70% in the last 15 years, although a significant disparity exists between households headed by older whites and older people of color. The highest median household income belongs to the 45 to 54-age bracket at $56,917. Older Americans, age 55 to 64, have a median income of $44,597, and those, age 65 to 74, a median income of $27,304.

Social security is the highest income source, accounting for 40% of total income. Pension, earnings and asset income account for approximately 20% each. It is projected that the aging population will work longer. Social security, pensions and tax laws will likely change significantly to accommodate delayed retirement. Income levels, as a result, are expected to increase. Demand for goods and services tailored to the elderly will soar in the future, creating millions of new service jobs.

Because women tend to outlive men, the female population has a good deal of disposable income. For many, houses and college fees are paid for, and children have left the nest. Many of these older "boomer" women will buy high dollar items like vacation homes, trips, cars, boats, wine cellars, golf equipment, etc. As grandmothers, they also purchase a significant amount of young children's apparel and toys.

## People with Disabilities

It is difficult to pinpoint with accuracy the purchasing power of this group due to reliance on self-identification. Estimates place aggregate income at over $1 trillion with purchasing power of approximately $220 billion. Contrary to pervasive assumptions, disabled persons spend money on travel (more than $80 billion a year) and on computers. More than any other constituency, people with disabilities often purchase cars with cash. One and a half million of the estimated eight million visually impaired persons own computers. With this group's substantial buying power, marketers would do well to design websites with them in mind. With 40% of this population using the Internet, service providers would be wise to market specifically to them.

People with disabilities are more likely to patronize businesses where they feel welcome and included. Accessibility to stores, products and services, including websites, will continue to have a major impact on this group's purchasing preferences. How people with disabilities respond to marketing efforts has an influence on the purchasing decisions of those closest to them, their families and friends.

## Next Generation Americans

In 2000, teens spent $155 billion, $2 billion more than the previous year. Children under the age of 18 are less likely to be white and twice as likely to be multiracial or multiethnic. This affords a great opportunity and challenge to companies in marketing their products to a group, which has a greater buying power and a higher level of pride in their multiculturalism than did their parents. Soft drink and retail apparel companies have been noteworthy marketers targeting this group, a virtual "cash-cow" opportunity.

## INCOME

Not only are people of color and multiethnic groups in the U. S. becoming more numerous, they are also becoming better educated, more visible and more demanding as customers as their affluence increases.

### Annual Median Income

| Group | Income |
|-------|--------|
| Seniors | $50,000 |
| Asian-Americans | $47,000 |
| Native Americans | $29,200 |
| Latinos | $26,600 |
| African-Americans | $26,000 |

Source: U.S. Bureau of Census
Money Income in the U.S., 1999

## MARKETING STRATEGIES

Many companies have learned a hard and expensive lesson in marketing to cultures about which they have too little knowledge. The opportunities for market share and lucrative profits by appealing to the ethnic markets here in the U.S., whose combined purchasing power has doubled over the last decade, are almost limitless. Customers are demanding that they be heard. In companies where there is substantial face-to-face and/or telephone contact with customers, sales and market share can increase significantly when customers can see that the people serving them understand their unique needs.

## Lessons Learned

By the same token, customer contact of a negative nature can have serious repercussions on the bottom line. As *Dillard's*, a leading retailer in the U.S., learned, sales and marketing efforts can be undermined when customers are not valued or treated with respect; then complain and are not heard. In this case, their complaints had to do with customer mistreatment and overly aggressive security measures implemented to prevent shoplifting. These measures appeared to target people of color disproportionately, and they complained vociferously. The resulting publicity had significant negative impact on customer loyalty and sales. The fall-out from the publicity was also very costly, creating a significant challenge to winning this customer base back.

It is no longer sufficient to dub English commercials into Spanish with lip movements out of synch. Translating print ads word for word also no longer works. *General Motors* learned that lesson in South America when they tried marketing the Nova automobile to that audience. If they had only known that "nova" in Spanish means "no go!"

Being unfamiliar with regional slang can result in ads offensive to the targeted culture. Take the example of *Perdue*, a poultry company. The owner stated in the ad, "it takes a tough man to make a tender chicken." In translation into Spanish it became, "it takes a sexually aroused man to make a chick affectionate!"

Using foreign words and not understanding their meaning, as one Japanese manufacturer of t-shirts learned, can be disastrous. The English words used on the shirt being manufactured turned out to be a lewd "four-letter" word, much to the company's embarrassment.

Pictures on products convey different messages to different cultures. Many cultures in sub-Saharan Africa identify the contents of a jar or a container literally by its picture. *Gerber* Baby Food features a (white) adorable baby on its jars. For obvious reasons, Africans refused to buy it.

A newly built casino in Las Vegas recently had to take down at considerable expense, a beautiful arch that all patrons were expected to walk under upon entering the establishment. The problem? Asians refused to enter, believing it was bad luck to walk under an arch. Much to the casino's dismay, they lost many Asian customers and their money at their grand opening.

Just as companies have had to learn how important it is to develop a substantive understanding of different cultures abroad in order to sell product, they are just beginning to recognize how they have ignored the fastest growing and most profitable market in the U.S., the ethnic market. In 1998, media marketing companies spent $200 billion advertising wares here in the U.S. Of that, under $2 billion, or less than 1%, was spent on targeting the ethnic market, which comprises 25% of the total consumer market. This represents significant missed opportunities.

## The Opportunistic...

*Walmart* and *Target* have made substantial effort to improve their service to ethnic communities. Perhaps encouraged by a number of allegations of discrimination, Wal-Mart requires, when possible, that people of color manage stores with predominantly diverse customers. Target employs a strategy in selecting merchandise that is appealing to its ethnic customers. Since 30% of *Mervyns'*, a Target Corporation subsidiary, clients are Latinos, it produces ads in both English and Spanish.

Despite its recent difficult times, *K-Mart*, recognizing that one-third of its customers are Latinos and African-Americans, is trying to further penetrate those markets as part of their strategy to recover from Chapter 11. African-Americans spend 87% more than whites at K-Mart; Latinos 40% more. K-Mart hired film director, Spike Lee, to shoot television spots for them in an effort to target the ethnic market.

Banks are also learning the importance of having tellers that reflect the diversity of their customers. ATM machines now offer services in Spanish, Russian and various Asian languages.

There are many examples of progressive companies beginning to target the underserved multicultural markets here in the U.S. Following are just a sample:

- Grocery stores in California, the *Tianguis* chain, cater to first-generation and Mexican immigrants, offering meats that are imported from Mexico.

- *J.C. Penney* offers a line of African apparel in its catalogs.

- To attract previously under-served populations in its San Francisco office, *Dreyfus* began offering sales information in Chinese and Spanish.

- In California, *Prodigy* launched *Prodigy en Espanol*, the first bilingual Internet service aimed at Latinos.[35]

- *Bud Light* featured an ad with two men holding hands and a slogan that appealed to the gay community, "Be Yourself and Make it a Bud Light."

- *Subaru*, appealing to the gay audience, ran an ad stating, "It's Not a Choice. It's the Way We're Built." Martina Navratilova, who is openly gay, has been a spokesperson.

- *SBC* cornered the market on Asian-Americans and Latinos residing in California and Texas, two of its largest markets, when it learned these groups were prepared to spend $65 billion on phone and Internet service.

- *Google*, the Internet search engine, recently expanded its search capabilities into Japanese, Chinese and Korean.

- *Merrill Lynch* opened a financial-services center for high income Asian-Americans in San Francisco, where they earn a median income of $61,000 and where Chinese-American senior executives and entrepreneurs run more than 2,000 Bay Area companies, worth more than $13 billion in revenues.

- *Johnson & Johnson* has cornered three-quarters of the Asian-American market for its Tylenol pain reliever and cold and allergy medications.

- *Outback*, recognizing that it had no restaurants that catered primarily to African-Americans, opened its first establishment in Prince George's County, Maryland, where a high concentration of African-Americans reside.

- Realizing that Latinos lagged behind other groups in the use of credit cards, *MasterCard* created a special outreach program offering education in money management to that sector of the population.

- *Ford* learned early on of the rewards to be gleaned by segmenting the U. S. multicultural markets. Their efforts have paid off handsomely: last year African-Americans alone, spent over $40 million on new and used Ford vehicles.

- *Avon's* CEO, Andrea Jung, pushed for the current corporate tag, "the company for women." Realizing that Avon's clientele were working and middle-class customers who desired, but couldn't afford, more elegant cosmetics; she directed the redesign and repackaging of product containers to create a more modern and sophisticated look. To better understand the selling experience and how to position business strategy most effectively, she went door-to-door in her neighborhood pushing her products and garnering feedback from neighbors.

- *Wells Fargo* recently made a $1 billion loan commitment to assist Latino small businesses.

- *National City Corporation* opened up a home loan business specifically for African-Americans, the group that has historically been underserved and rejected most for mortgages.[36]

- Instead of Big Macs, *McDonald's* has begun offering Ozburgers in Australia, wiener schnitzels in Germany and Lamb McSpicy's in the U.K.

Seemingly small and subtle changes to a multicultural marketing campaign can often yield significant results.

## Acquisitions

One strategy some companies have employed to tap into and expand their ethnic market share are acquisitions of multicultural businesses. There has been an explosion of small media businesses started by people of color - magazines, radio stations, television and Internet sites. It is not surprising then that acquisitions have been most apparent in the entertainment and media sectors.

*Viacom* spent $3 million for *Black Entertainment Television (BET),* and it gained over 60 million loyal viewers by so doing. *Time Inc.* became the first mainstream publisher to acquire a major multiethnic publication, *Essence,* with over seven million readers. *AOL* now owns *Africana.com,* a website popular with African-Americans for its focus on history and culture.

## Segmentation

Another marketing strategy that is crucial to a company's success in breaking into the ethnic markets here in the U.S. is segmentation. An ad geared toward women does not necessarily appeal to **all** women. Consumers can't be treated as a homogeneous group. There are young women, older women, single women, married women, middle-aged homemakers, lesbian women and women of color. Similarly, to try and appeal to all Latino sub-groups by marketing in English only or Spanish only will not produce desired results.

Healthcare, financial services and household goods are consumed differently by women of varying backgrounds. Women of color are demanding different products than standard issue. No longer do African-American women have to "make do" with flesh-colored band-aids or suntan shades of cosmetics. *Revlon, Maybelline and Estee Lauder* have recognized the tremendous rate of return on marketing to women of color. Standard mainstream cosmetic products are barely growing at 3% annually, while new lines targeting women of color are seeing increased sales of 25% per year. Women of color can now purchase greeting cards, Barbies and Santa Clauses that reflect their color and culture.

Marketing segmentation is also most important when appealing to the Asian-American consumers. Because their umbrella comprises so many national ancestries and such diverse cultures, niche marketing is advised, creating distinct ads to address the specific needs of each subgroup: Chinese, Filipino, Japanese, Asian-Indians, Korean, and Vietnamese.[37]

Mainstream marketing is not effective with cultural sub-groups. "One size fits all" advertising strategies succeeded when the U. S. was thought to be a monolithic, Anglo-dominated market. The trend in America has changed dramatically toward greater cultural, ethnic and linguistic diversity.

Companies that market successfully to the U.S. multicultural market often find that the same product preferences play well globally in the Pacific Rim and South America, where there is a pent up consumer demand for U.S. goods. For some companies, it works in the reverse, where products offered to diverse global markets also tend to provide valuable insight to ethnic markets here in the U.S. As the diversity within the marketing and advertising industry expands, so will its capability to market more effectively to meet the needs of a growing diverse customer base, both globally and domestically.

What is clear is that the failure of companies to recognize the growing afflu-ence and increasing demographics of the emerging markets here in the U.S. will prove to be a missed opportunity and worse, a costly mistake.

## CHALLENGES & OPPORTUNITIES

The opportunities are almost limitless for market share and lucrative profits of the ethnic markets in the U. S., whose combined purchasing power has doubled over the last decade. The challenge for marketers is first, to target this market, and secondly, to design cost-effective campaigns that hit the right targets. The American Advertising Foundation has developed some proactive recommended practices to assist advertising and marketing firms in maximiz-ing the benefits of diversity and inclusion throughout the process. This means that marketers must understand the values, perceptions, product require-ments, purchasing preferences and trends of the multiethnic, multicultural U.S. market. It also means that marketing is not just about giving customers what they *say* they want. It's trying to understand exactly what they *do* want by asking the right questions, which requires a deeper understanding of the culture.

Customer service is about delighting the customers and being able to antici-pate their needs. If your customers are strangers, they won't be your customers for long. Ideally, you want your customers to be your advertisers. Word-of-mouth advertising (viral marketing) is often the most compelling.

Another challenge in attracting a multicultural market is that of increasing brand loyalty. Most ethnic constituencies in the U.S. are brand conscious. However, with the exception of gays and lesbians, they are not typically brand loyal. Effective multicultural marketing and excellence in customer service can improve this.

Part of a sound marketing plan will likely have to include a shared database of consumer preferences by global regions and domestic multicultural mar-kets. This strategy will help indicate where needs coincide and where pitfalls exist. Managing the dynamics between local and global initiatives will be a major challenge.

## CONCLUSION

Companies that intend to be competitive going forward must understand and aggressively court emerging market customers, including people of color, women, gays, people with disabilities, the aging and next generation. No matter how complex business gets, it will always be a game of supply and demand. In the U.S., diversity markets remain the best growth opportunity around. That's where the new money is, and that is where it will continue to be.

A well-thought out marketing plan targeting the ethnic market doesn't begin with advertising, however. It begins with the company's strategy of having diversity represented in its ranks that will better relate, better understand and better serve these customers. Otherwise, this customer base will go to competitors where they see a reflection of themselves and feel valued, comfortable and wanted.

SUMMARY HIGHLIGHTS
# Business Imperative 3: Emerging Customer Base

- Middle-class consumers are emerging globally. By 2010 Eastern Europe, Asia (excluding Japan) and Latin America will increase their share of purchasing power to one-third of the world's total.

- Women-owned businesses are increasing dramatically worldwide. They need to be taken seriously as a major player in the emerging global markets.

- Populating teams with the diversity of emerging markets, enabling them to relate to and think like the customer as well as better understand and predict how products and advertising will play out in those cultures, is a smart business decision.

- If the purchasing power of ethnic Americans were represented separately, it would be the sixth largest market in the world.

- Minority spending power is growing 65% faster than U.S. purchasing power overall.

- Purchasing power of the multicultural American market has increased dramatically. Taken as an aggregate, it would be the third largest market in the world after the U.S. and Japan:

  - Aging Americans:              $900 billion
  - African-Americans:           $646 billion
  - Latinos:                     $581 billion
  - LGBT:                        $514 billion
  - Asian-Americans:             $296 billion
  - People with Disabilities:    $220 billion
  - Next Generation Americans:   $155 billion
  - Native Americans:            $ 41 billion

- American women are the largest economic force on the planet, controlling $5.2 trillion.

- Customer service is about delighting customers and being able to anticipate their needs. If your customers are strangers, they won't be your customers for long.

# BUSINESS IMPERATIVE #4:

## THE WAR
## FOR TALENT

We are in a war for talent. And the only way you can meet your business imperatives is to have all people as part of your talent pool - here in the United States and around the world

> -   Rich McGinn, Past CEO[38]
>     Lucent Technologies

# THE CRISIS

In 1998, the McKinsey Company came out with their exhaustive and illuminating research entitled, *The War for Talent*. Focusing primarily on the shortage of executive talent, the findings suggested that in order to win this war; Corporate America must elevate it to a burning priority.[39] The same level of attention and accountability needs to be applied to the overall shrinking labor force America now faces. This critical shortage of skilled workers has become a business emergency. The dearth of qualified people especially at the highest skill level has given birth to an all-out war for the best and the brightest.

In June 2000, *Business Week* predicted there would be a significant increase in the technical labor shortage in the U.S. by 2002, namely one million workers.[40] This number is four times higher than the shortage realized in 1998 of a quarter of a million workers. The Business Higher Education Forum found that by 2028 there will be 19 million more jobs here in the U.S. than workers to fill them. About 40% of the people available to fill the jobs will be minority. This represents a steeper decline in fewer workers by an additional 15% than what we have today, which is estimated to be a 10% disparity. *Time Magazine* noted that the birth rate per 1,000 Americans is at its lowest level since the government began keeping records in 1909.[41] This ensures a tight job market for decades to come.

The California Council on Science and Technology warns there is no quick fix for the problem. "There is a widening 'gap' between the state's workforce needs and the educational system's ability to respond." The supply and demand curves are going in just the wrong directions. By the year 2030, it is predicted that 60% of Texans will have only a high school diploma or less.

U.S. Secretary of Labor, Elaine Chao, says that the U.S. is transitioning into a high-skilled, information-based economy. "This has created a disconnect between the jobs that are being created and the current skills of many workers."

The social contract that promised job security in exchange for employee loyalty has been dissolved. Corporate restructuring abounds. Work that is not deemed to be a core competency is being outsourced to temporary, contract workers. The contingent workforce is growing at a rate of 30% a year. If this trend continues, half of the workforce could be contract in a few short years; employed as part-time and full-time "leased" employees. Many of these highly skilled workers will be self-employed. *Manpower*, the temporary staffing company, is now one of the largest employers in the U.S. The implications for business are the loss of control over these workers and the challenge of recruiting, retaining and managing a temporary workforce that will tend to be loyal to the work they are doing, not necessarily to the company.

And the labor shortage is not relegated just to the U.S. Europe has been experiencing a draught in workers as well. Britain has set up a skills shortage national task force to address the issue. Businesses located in Asia are competitively vying for talent, particularly technical talent, especially with the "brain drain" they experience as some of their best and brightest are recruited to work here in the U.S. Nor are the effects of the labor shortage being felt just by large companies. Small businesses are finding it increasingly difficult to hire talent, facing a dire choice of leaving the job unfilled or hiring someone less than qualified.

The adverse impact of the labor shortage is profound. When there are too few workers, companies are forced to offer higher wages and better benefits in order to competitively attract talent. If equivalent productivity improvements aren't realized, profits suffer and inflation sets in.

## A SHRINKING SKILLED LABOR FORCE

There are a number of reasons why the skilled workforce in the U.S. is shrinking:

- Decline in birth rates, particularly amongst Caucasians. The supply of available 35 to 44 year-olds to fill top slots has just begun a 15% decline. There are simply not enough GenXers to make up the loss of baby boomers beginning to retire.

- Slow growth of one percent in number of job seekers, compared to a job growth rate of 14%.

- Bulk of job creation and economic growth is in the service area, demanding higher skills.

- Failure of public education to prepare the emerging labor force with proper basic skill development to perform entry-level jobs.

- Skills required to perform even entry-level jobs have continuously been upgraded.

- Emerging workforce is increasingly comprised of people of color and immigrants, with whom educational parity and the ability to move upward in the workforce is most at risk.

- Low skill, lower-paying jobs are on the decline. Job demand will not keep up with the glut of unskilled workers.

- Competition for talent extends beyond the borders of the U.S. It now exists with all participants in the global economy, many of whom are upgrading skills faster than the U.S.

- New entrants to the U.S. workforce with skills in math and science, already a scarcity, do not compete on par with some of their global peers. The result is that U.S. firms prefer foreign workers, and reliance on hiring them has increased.

- The nation's unemployment rate, in spite of the recent recession and rash of corporate lay-offs, is very low, increasing the challenge of finding qualified workers.

- The loss of the most experienced and skilled workers, the baby boomers, that are beginning to retire.

The current and future labor pool is not only shrinking but will be more brown, black and gray.

## EFFECTS OF DEMOGRAPHICS ON THE WORKFORCE

The percentage of males in the U. S. workforce has decreased from 88% in 1950 to slightly over 50% today. It's not that white males are no longer new entrants. They are. However, the number of white male baby boomers who are retiring is greater than white male new entrants. In fact,

> *People of color, women, older workers and immigrants now comprise two-thirds of the U.S. workforce.*

By 2005, the Department of Labor projects that 51% of net new entrants to the workforce will be people of color and 62% will be women. The U.S.

workforce currently grows by approximately 1.5 million workers a year. According to the Department of Labor, each year approximately 500,000 legal immigrants and 250,000 illegal immigrants are added to that number. Over the last decade minorities have grown to more than half of the net new entrants[42] into the workforce, 85% of whom are immigrants.

This trend will continue to be so in the future. New immigrants were responsible for 25% of the workforce growth in the 1980s and doubled their numbers a decade later!

The number of dual-income families continues to rise. In 2000, approximately 80% of all school-age children (70% of pre-school children) had mothers working outside the home or seeking work. For the first time, the generation of Americans born after 1964 will spend more time caring for aging parents than children.

The increase in aging workers is perhaps the *most* significant trend in the labor market today. During the next 30 years, the number of 65 and older potential workers will double to nearly 70 million.

## ECONOMIC FACTORS AFFECTING JOBS

The Hudson Institute predicts that a rapidly changing economy will harm low-skilled and poorly educated workers here in the U.S. who don't adapt to changes in the workplace. Their jobs and wages will continue to be at risk. What are the forces shaping our economy? Why is this so?

### Technology Breakthroughs

Technological breakthroughs, particularly in I.T., computing and wireless telecommunications, tend to reduce the demand for lower skilled workers while increasing the efficiency of operation. For example, technology has reduced the need for bank tellers, telephone operators and some manufacturing jobs. Yet, technology has usually created more jobs than it reduces, primarily in the development and management of technology. Consider that two of the fastest growing professions, software development and website design, did not even exist until the late 1980s. Technology has increased the speed of doing business, shortened product life cycles and accelerated competition, but it will *not* make the labor shortage go away.

## Globalization

Globalization increases the consumption of imported goods and services produced by low-skilled workers overseas. As a result, the demand for similarly produced goods and services here in the U.S. will be significantly reduced. An advantage of globalization to the U.S. is the ability to specialize in producing the goods and services in which we command the greatest comparative advantage, such as machinery, vehicles, scientific equipment and pharmaceuticals. This, in turn, helps us raise incomes and living standards in America, at least for those workers who have been flexible and adaptable in acquiring the skills needed in these specialized sectors.

## Skill Requirements

Workers with the skills needed to do these jobs and even higher level skilled jobs, particularly in the technical sectors, are in short supply. The war for talent has been most evident in the computer and semiconductor industries here in the U.S., where high-skilled jobs have been created very quickly and sometimes go unfilled. According to the National Science Foundation, 80% of the increase in engineering jobs will occur in computer-related fields. In fact, employment in these occupations across all industries is expected to double by 2008, with over one million jobs being added.

The demand for foreign-born workers to supply the skill requirements in the high-tech sector has caused aggressive lobbying on the part of American companies to increase the number of U.S. work visas issued annually for technical positions. Paying for all of these green cards has proven to be a costly strategy for companies. Given heightened political tensions in the world, the likelihood that Congress will increase the quotas on foreign-born workers seems remote. The competition for home-grown technical talent will be exacerbated.

## Outsourcing

An alternative has been to outsource the work abroad. Some argue that much of the programming done for U.S.-based businesses has been outsourced to India. In reality much of the 24-hour customer-service-line work is moving to English-speaking countries around the world. The catalyst driving this trend is undoubtedly cost driven, but the shortage of qualified customer service workers is also a factor. Yet, there are some jobs that can't be outsourced overseas, such as security guards and cashiers, for which there will continue to be demand.

Outsourcing work, however, can be an expensive proposition. While the costs of labor may be cheaper, the infrastructure, such as establishing offices and communication networks, are not. Complying with employment laws in other countries can be challenging and expensive.

## Lower Unemployment

According to estimates of the Department of Labor, the unemployment rate could fall to 2% within a few short years. With all of the challenges that an increasingly diverse and shrinking labor force present, how will U.S. companies win the war for talent and maintain our competitive economy?

## IMPACT OF EDUCATION

Wages for low-skilled work are projected to fall, and new jobs requiring advanced technical skills will increase. This shift will have a rippling effect on communities and families dependent on the old economy. It will no longer suffice to have *the will* to work. Being well educated and possessing technical skills will become the new norm. As Ted Childs, Vice President of Diversity for IBM, states:

> For business it's [the labor shortage] a survival issue. We need educated people to work for us and to be our customers. And we need strong, vibrant, healthy communities as places to do business. Both of these depend on giving all our people real access to a quality education.[43]

As *Opportunity 2000* reminded us, a gap exists between what skills companies need to succeed in a global economy and what a failing public education system in the U.S. equips workers to do. There is a major disconnect between curriculum developers in public education and the requisite skills in the marketplace. A systematic approach to incorporating into the curriculum changes in job responsibilities and skills required to perform even the most entry-level positions is lacking. Today, most entry-level jobs in major companies require, at the very least, a high school diploma and in many cases an associate's degree. The Department of Labor predicts this trend will continue.

*Workforce 2020* points out that skills and education strongly influence income levels here in the U.S.[44] As would be expected, high school graduates saw their earnings increase marginally, while the earnings of high school drop-outs failed to keep up with inflation. Similarly, recipients of college degrees have, on the average, outpaced the income of those without a degree.

The average earnings of whites significantly exceed those of African-Americans and Latinos. While African-Americans are increasing their earning power more rapidly than whites, Latinos are lagging due to little improvement in educational attainment.

Unless the education and skill levels of the American worker are upgraded, our ability to increase productivity and grow the economy at required rates will be in jeopardy. Because the workforce will grow slowly, desired economic growth will no longer be achieved simply by adding more workers. Those workers are no longer available. Instead, worker productivity must increase, which requires improved education and technology.

## FUTURE TALENT PIPELINE

By 2020, most minority workers will continue to be less well educated than white counterparts. Educational improvement is most pressing for people of color in this country, particularly Latinos.

### High School Pipeline

While the enrollment in high schools has decreased due to declining birth rates, some of the groups whose populations are projected to grow the most over the next decades are the very groups who suffer the worst attrition. Currently, people of color make up 33% of the nation's school-age population. By 2035, this percentage will grow to 50%. Latino representation has increased 58% in the last decade. In Texas, Latinos will become the majority group by 2020. Yet, their drop-out rate, which includes foreign-born Latinos, continues to be approximately 40% nationwide.

According to the Census Bureau, the most recent data on high school graduation rates is from 1998:

## High School Graduation Rates, 1998

|                   | Male | Female |
|-------------------|------|--------|
| African-American  | 65%  | 77%    |
| Asian-American    | 87%  | 88%    |
| White             | 78%  | 83%    |
| Latino            | 50%  | 62%    |

Source: U.S. Census, 2000

This represents little change for whites and Latinos over the past twenty years, while graduation rates for African-Americans have improved 10%. Asian-American graduation rates remain the highest. Women graduate more often than men in all groups. If these trends continue, it will take Latinos approximately 60 years to reach parity with white high school graduation rates! Research on the state of education provided to Latinos suggests that there are many leaks along all levels of their educational pipeline. As the National Action Council for Minorities in Engineering (NACME) observes, "at every point of this pipeline, from high school to advanced degrees, Latinos lose ground."[45]

Some of the reasons for this disparity include:

• School districts with high percentages of minority students have lower expenditures because of lower revenue.

• Minority students are disproportionately placed in lower track courses, decreasing their access to higher education.

• The more poorly prepared teachers tend to be employed by schools with higher percentages of minorities. In California alone, 40,000 teachers are under-qualified, working with emergency permits or waivers instead of formal credentials.

• Latinos have higher incidences of language barriers. Their culture also places value on young adults contributing to family finances at the expense of finishing school.

- A large number of immigrants completed little formal education before emigrating here. Over a decade ago, foreign-born individuals accounted for more than 20% of all U.S. residents without a high school degree. Today, only 44% of foreign-born Latino adults are high school graduates (compared to 70% of U.S.-born Latino adults).

- Parents of today's minority youth often have less formal education than their counterparts. A student's academic performance is often influenced by the educational level of his/her parents.

If we are to fill skilled jobs in this country even at the lowest level, the need to improve graduation rates amongst people of color is critical. The disparity in the quality of education for people of color in this country also needs to be addressed. High schools must teach curricula that reflect the requirements of industry and enable students to enter the workforce with the necessary skills. Until people of color have access to higher education in numbers equal to their demographics, their skills and abilities will be sub-optimized. Research shows that 10% more education equates to 8.6% improvement in productivity.

There is evidence that SAT scores are improving for people of color. A decade ago Asian-Americans began surpassing SAT scores of white students. Over the past 20 years, African-Americans have increased their scores by 58 points and Latinos by 21 points, compared to only two points for white counterparts. Without proactive intervention, it will take some time for most minority students to attain SAT equivalence with whites.

American students are consistently beaten in international competition, the fiercest of which comes from Asia. When compared with foreign students, no population group in the U.S. performs in competitions nearly as well. U.S. students score below the world average in math. Only 10% of America's math students match the scores of students from Singapore, the global leader. 12th graders have a low level of math and science proficiency.

Not only are American students poorly prepared for careers in science and engineering, many of them are simply not interested in engineering or technology. The U.S. ranks below many major industrialized and emerging countries in the proportion of its college-age population with engineering degrees.

## # B.S. Degrees in Engineering

Country                                    %

China . . . . . . . . . . . . . . . . . . . . . 46%
Germany . . . . . . . . . . . . . . . . . . . 33%
Russia . . . . . . . . . . . . . . . . . . . . . 32%
Singapore . . . . . . . . . . . . . . . . . . 30%
Taiwan . . . . . . . . . . . . . . . . . . . . 21%
Japan . . . . . . . . . . . . . . . . . . . . . 20%
Colombia . . . . . . . . . . . . . . . . . . 20%
Syria . . . . . . . . . . . . . . . . . . . . . . 19%
Mexico . . . . . . . . . . . . . . . . . . . . 18%
Cuba . . . . . . . . . . . . . . . . . . . . . . 16%
UK . . . . . . . . . . . . . . . . . . . . . . . . 9%
Canada . . . . . . . . . . . . . . . . . . . . 7%
U.S. . . . . . . . . . . . . . . . . . . . . . . . 5%

Source: National Science Foundation Science & Engineering 2000

This table underscores the low priority given in the U.S. to the study of engineering and should present a sense of urgency to those who wish to address the issues of a shortage of technical workers.[46]

## College Pipeline

More than ever, the key to a skilled job and economic security is higher education. Not only is college graduation important, but the choice of degree is as well. Generic degrees are not in demand, and the pursuit of such a degree does not guarantee a higher income. The demand is for engineering, computer science, math, science and, to a lesser extent, business and liberal arts degrees.

Since 1980, the size of the college-age population has declined by 21%, contributing to the overall decline in enrollments. While this trend is expected to reverse by 2010, a significant number of college-age persons at that time will be people of color, some of whom are considered "at risk" students. African-Americans, Native Americans and especially Latinos are less likely than Asians and whites to graduate from high school, enroll in college and graduate. Our ability to meet the growing demand of technical jobs will be tied to our success in preparing and educating this emerging population in math and science.

## General Enrollment

With the exception of women and Asian-Americans, enrollment in colleges and universities for all populations has remained flat over the past four years. Forty-four percent of Asian-Americans have Bachelors degrees, compared to 26% of the total population. African-American women and Latinas are more likely than males in their groups to attend college. Together, people of color make up 28% of the undergraduate population in colleges and universities. In 2000, they received slightly less than 22% of all degrees, an increase of almost 6% in one year. As a percentage of their own group, graduation rates are as follows:

### College Graduation Rate as a % of Group

| Group | % |
|---|---|
| Whites | 48% |
| Asian-Americans | 47% |
| African-Americans | 34% |
| Latinos | 32% |

Source: National Science Foundation

The most popular degree amongst students of color is business with the exception of Asians, who contribute 10% of our engineering workforce.

## ENGINEERING ENROLLMENT

### People of Color

Over the next decade the need for bachelor-degreed technical professionals will grow almost twice as fast as the overall average. Yet, engineering enrollment has steadily declined since 1983. This is largely due to fewer whites enrolling, whose birth rate is also lower. On the positive side, enrollment in engineering programs for students of color has increased, albeit slightly, over the same period of time. This occurred in spite of enrollment of African-Americans dropping a whopping 16% from 1992-1997. According to the Engineering Workforce Commission, that trend began to reverse the following year.[47] Yet, participation rates of college-age African-Americans and

Latinos continue to remain at one-half the overall national rate, a further indication of their underrepresentation.

Since 1992, overall enrollment, including people of color, in graduate engineering programs has declined slightly. This is an important data point that is sometimes used to measure a nation's capacity for innovation.

Overall, the number of bachelors' degrees awarded in engineering has continued to decrease over the past decade. For people of color, there has been a very slight increase, in part due to the fact that half of all bachelors degrees earned by Asians are in science and engineering. Students of color obtain 12% of Bachelor's degrees, 5.7% of Master's degrees and 3.5% of doctorates in engineering.[48]

Fewer students of color complete their bachelor's degree within five years. This is due, in part, to their greater likelihood of having to hold down part-time jobs. More students of color than traditional students transfer out of engineering programs.

In the past, foreign students tended to inflate the percentage of students of color obtaining degrees in engineering in the U.S. Their numbers have decreased, dropping from 33% in 1992, to 3% in 1997. The number of doctorates obtained amongst this group has also declined by 15% in the same timeframe. Engineering education in Asian countries (China, in particular) are reducing their reliance on U.S. universities, particularly at the graduate level.

Although the trend of African-Americans and Latinos graduating with bachelor's degrees in engineering is slightly positive, the relative number remains *very low*, less than five percent each. Some of the reasons cited for this include financial difficulty, poor preparation for college, limiting support groups and role models, and lower expectations on the part of parents and faculty. Access to skills that higher education provides continues to be a national crisis for people of color in this country.

## Women

Even though the rate of females likely to enter college versus males is 70.3% to 63.5% respectively, women are less likely than men to choose engineering as a major. The percentage of women receiving bachelors' degrees in engineering continues to be much lower than men, about 18%. Slow progress has been made over the past decade except in computer science. Today, 27% of computer science degrees are awarded to women. That figure should cause little comfort, however, as it represents an alarming 10% drop from 15 years ago. As low as these numbers are in proportion to their demographics, U.S. women lead the world in the number of degrees earned in engineering and computer science. By comparison, Japanese women earned 8% and 23% respectively. Currently though, women are making significant strides in obtaining undergraduate and graduate degrees in science (which includes natural, social and behavioral sciences).

Overall, these educational trends offer little cause for optimism, especially for African-Americans and Latinos. This data suggests that while the demand for bachelor's degrees in engineering and computer science is projected to increase significantly, people of color and women continue to be under-represented in these fields. This is especially alarming when projected populations, particularly for people of color, will dramatically increase. There is a serious need *now* for greater participation by women and people of color to pursue engineering degrees in numbers that match their demographics.

Citing the low level of participation of people of color in both higher education and the workplace, a coalition of CEOs and university Presidents recently convened to brainstorm recommendations for significant change to address this national crisis. They proposed the following:

- Support and strengthen programs to teach students the value of higher education, how to apply for college and obtain scholarships.

- Provide resources to prepare teachers to work with diverse students.

- Advocate that colleges and universities consider qualities of student applicants beyond their test scores.

- Urge national policy makers to increase funding of federal education grants for students.

- Encourage participation of corporate foundations in the effort.

In my opinion, these proposals don't go far enough. My recommendations are discussed below.

## CHALLENGES AND OPPORTUNITIES

The persistent gap in educational attainment is linked to experiences in elementary and secondary school. Many African-American, Latino and Native American students do not take advanced science and math courses that prepare students for higher education in technical fields. The disparity between white and minority students will remain significant. Given increasing diversity and a decreasing number of skilled workers, it will take an aggressive budget allocation and comprehensive plan, including the following recommendations, to win the war for talent:

- Training for middle school and high school teachers needs to improve to upgrade their current skill set, especially in acquiring technological literacy. The certification process needs to be standardized and rigorously enforced. Teacher pay needs to be increased significantly, particularly when they have participated in skills upgrade training. Additional sourcing and teacher pipeline strategies need to be developed to attract underutilized populations into teaching, such as aging workers or retirees, many of whom would make excellent educators.

- Primary and secondary education needs to set high and uniform standards on teaching the *basics*: math, science, reasoning ability, reading, writing, computer skills and English, enabling the emerging workforce to be upwardly mobile. Public education needs to be held accountable for results.

- The federal government must increase the number of vouchers and charter schools that give options to parents in the educating of their children.

- Colleges need to assume more responsibility for understanding the needs of industry and coaching students in making wise decisions regarding selecting a major that provides requisite skills and income.

- A national campaign needs to be implemented to inform students early on of what science and engineering are really about and to change the image of engineering from being sterile, dull and conservative to one of being a powerful force that improves quality of life globally.

- Information on labor market trends, career development, skill acquisition and educational opportunities needs to be collected by a designated government entity on a systematic and continuous basis. This information needs to be made readily accessible to educational institutions and workers wanting to upgrade their skills.

In addition to educational initiatives, recommendations for Corporate America's involvement to offset the skills shortage include:

- Create ways to attract an underutilized and growing segment of our population, the aging worker, to fill the skill shortage. This will include lobbying for substantive changes to Social Security, Medicare, health insurance and taxes that currently make it unfavorable for older workers to remain in the work force.

- Companies need to develop strategies to tap into other pipelines of underutilized talents such as people with disabilities, of whom only 56% of those able to work are actually working; and stay-at-home parents for whom an alternative work schedule might be appealing. Training former welfare recipients is another. Some companies are even exploring training former criminals, 80% of whom are incarcerated for non-violent crimes.

- Enlightened immigration policies that give preference to skilled workers, not unskilled, will be needed. Lower-skilled immigrants will continue to require remedial training in basic skills.

- Corporate America needs to step up its remedial training for workers in basic and academic skills as well as "retooling" courses that replace obsolete skills.

- Overall, companies will need to manage workplace skills with the same kind of attention they pay to market signals. This will require greater priority being given to skills training and an improved ability in matching workers to jobs.

- With an increase in women and dual-career families in the workplace, more work/life programs that address balance issues need to be offered.

- Companies that serve their communities in partnerships to improve public education become the employer of choice for their constituencies. Awarding scholarships, internships and work-study programs aimed at students and teachers as incentives to keep students in high school and college or to keep teachers apprised of requisite skill needs is good business.

- Corporate America needs to step up its support for increasing diversity in colleges and universities, where collective cultural competence can begin and where a diversity pipeline for future leaders can be developed.

- Companies will need to address the issue of creating a sense of belonging, promoting affiliation and community in their organizations to counter the forces of isolation and disloyalty that are characteristic of the new business unit, dispersed multi-national teams, contingency workers and telecommuters.

## CONCLUSION

> Numerous studies point out that the U.S. ... is not prepared ...[with]... the skills necessary for success in the digital economy. From lagging scores on standardized testing to a growing chasm in access to and comfort with technology, the issue of skills development ...[becomes of]... primary concern as employers face increased global competition for goods, services and labor.[50]

The shortage of skilled labor is here and will only get worse in the future. A commitment to educating our future pipeline of talent about the need for engineers and scientists must begin now.

Early education is the most cost-effective way to manage the negative trend of unskilled youth in the future. If the U.S. will stand up to the task of increasing the number of high school graduates with appropriate skills, it could go a long way toward filling available jobs and laying a suitable foundation on which workers could upgrade their skills once in the workforce.

Full participation of people of color in the workforce and the effects this has on other aspects of life is increasingly important to the U.S. Our ability to succeed in this global economy and maintain our standard of living depends on it.

Companies cannot simply wait for people of color to flood the workplace. If they don't invest in educating today's underrepresented minorities through public sector initiatives, these citizens won't be prepared to be tomorrow's productive workers and future leaders.

In the past, a blue-collar worker could make a decent living without higher education so long as he/she passed the high school equivalency test. Today, if a person can't write, communicate, calculate, think, reason, use sound judgment and make good decisions, his/her employment outlook is bleak. Since public education is not getting the job done, companies will have to play a larger role.

In order for employers to win the war for talent, they will need to be creative in designing recruiting strategies and retaining their workers.

> To attract and retain such talented workers for their firms, employers will need to accommodate their desires. Older workers are likely to want to be able to work at home a few days each month. Women (and men) with young children will be attracted by "family friendly" policies such as flexible scheduling, job sharing, and on-site or subsidized daycare. Companies that provide such flexibility...will...be able to attract and retain qualified workers without paying as much in salary and traditional benefits as other companies that do not cater to such specific needs.[51]

These kinds of arrangements will be in much greater demand in the future than they have been in the past as the percentage of telecommuters, part-timers and contingent workers increase. The IT revolution will only cause this trend to grow.

## SUMMARY HIGHLIGHTS
# Business Imperative 4: War for Talent

- The technical labor shortage today in the U.S. is estimated to be one million.

- The supply and demand curve of projected jobs vs. projected workers is going in the wrong direction.

- People of color, women, older workers and immigrants now comprise two-thirds of the U.S. workforce.  These numbers will continue to increase.

- The current and projected increase in aging workers is perhaps the most significant trend in the labor market today.

- Wages for low-skilled work are projected to fall, and new jobs requiring advanced technical skills will increase.  This shift will have a significant effect on communities and families dependent on the old economy.

- Unless lower-skilled American workers are retooled with new skills, their ability to  provide for their families and survive financially will be at risk.  The U.S.'s ability to increase productivity and grow the economy at required rates will also be in jeopardy.

- Only ten percent of America's math students match the scores of students from Singapore, the global leader.

- Twenty-two percent of first-year engineering students in this country need remediation in math and/or science.

- The U.S. ranks below many major industrialized and emerging countries in the proportion of its college-age population graduating with engineering degrees.

- Over the next decade the need for bachelor-degreed technical professionals will grow almost twice as fast as the overall average.

- Asian countries are reducing their reliance on engineering education in U.S. universities, particularly at the graduate level.

- With the exception of Asians, who contribute ten percent of our engineers, the number of engineering degrees earned by people of color remains extremely low.

- The percentage of women receiving bachelors' degrees in engineering continues to be much lower than men.

- There is a serious need now for greater participation by women and people of color to pursue engineering degrees in numbers that match their demographics.

- Flexible work arrangements will be in much greater demand in the future as the percentage of telecommuters, part-timers and contingent workers increase.

# BUSINESS IMPERATIVE #5:

## IMPROVING BUSINESS COMPETENCIES

### Recruitment ~ Retention ~ Supplier Procurement

Supplier diversity programs help to create more businesses, more entrepreneurship, more employment, and more business training ... Strengthening communities by reaching out to diverse suppliers has been a cornerstone of [our] business policy for more than 20 years. By learning to reach out to diverse suppliers, we also learn to reach out to diverse customers.[52]

- Geoffrey C. Bible, Chairman
  Philip Morris Companies

## RECRUITMENT

A commitment to and excellence in executing a diversity recruiting strategy is no longer optional for companies that want to compete successfully for talent. A recent survey conducted by the Society of Human Resource Management (SHRM) found that 62% of job seekers prefer to work for a company with a demonstrated commitment to diversity.[53]

In today's competitive market, it makes little sense to recruit from only part of the talent pipeline - a pipeline that is already short on skilled workers. Every organization wants to hire the best and brightest people. Not recognizing the importance of recruiting from the entire spectrum of candidates is missing an opportunity.

Recruiting costs will increase dramatically if companies contend only for the increasingly smaller pool of non-diverse candidates. If unemployment rates continue to be low, failing to recruit from an increasing segment of the population will have a direct impact on the level of talent in the company. If companies fail to recruit diverse talent, their competitors will.

Hiring individuals that are representative of an organization's customer base and the communities in which it operates is good business practice. In a global economy companies can hire "remote workers," and import talent, but global recruiting requires managers and recruiters with global intelligence, skills and diverse experiences and perspectives. Non-diverse employees are even demanding a more diverse workforce in their companies, and "activist" stockholders often question the firm's position on diversity at stockholder meetings.

One of the key indicators as to how committed a company is to diversity is in its recruiting effort. The numbers tell the story. Companies must plan for the future by recruiting talent, including diverse candidates, who, with development, will become the next leaders of the company. Most organizations fill leadership positions internally through promotions and/or succession planning. If supplying the pipeline is neglected, creating diversity at higher levels in the organization down the road will be much more challenging.

Perpetuating a leadership style and set of beliefs that mirrors the background and mindsets of predecessors is not conducive to capitalizing on opportunities that diversity offers. A company that can identify the skills it will require to meet future needs, develop long-term strategies to meet these requirements and execute aggressively to plan, will be the true winners in the war for talent - *all* talent.

The last decade has seen significant activity in mergers, joint ventures and acquisitions. In some respects, this strategy has become an alternative to recruitment. Understanding the implications of diversity on these business alliances *up front* can help facilitate the transition and optimize the merging of two cultures into one to achieve joint business objectives. Many such alliances have not been successful due to failure in incorporating diversity and change management principles into the planning.

## What Candidates Look For

Why do great people join companies? Research tells us that candidates look for companies that are industry leaders with strong business models, multiple revenue streams and innovative products and services. They also look for organizations that are magnets for other talented people, where jobs are challenging and continuously "stretch" capability and where customer intimacy and the opportunity to "really make a difference" in the customers' lives are valued. People aren't motivated solely by money. Money is a way of keeping score.

Perhaps the most critical component for successfully attracting talent, especially diverse talent, is the culture of the organization. As the McKinsey Report states, the heart of a great company (its brand) is an "appealing culture and inspiring values."[54] Companies are evaluated on their openness to and affirmation of unique differences, ideas and problem solving. They look for a company where there is zero tolerance for anything less than absolute trust, unconditional acceptance and respect. If would-be employees don't feel that their background, competence and perspectives will be valued by an organization, or if they don't sense that their ideas and opinions will be given consideration, or if they don't perceive that they will be given an equal opportunity for successive positions of responsibility, they'll go elsewhere to an employer who exemplifies these attributes. It's the culture that's important. It's the company's commitment to operating in an environment that demands and demonstrates inclusion. It's the institutionalization of systems that promote development and opportunity for *all* employees.

Evidence of an organization's diversity has become a *major* selection criterion for would-be recruits. They judge companies on their commitment to diversity, often requesting evidence of role models in positions of power. They want to know how long it took for a person of color to reach a high level. Some even prefer reporting to diverse managers and make their decisions about joining a company based on this factor. A well thought out diversity initiative that is endorsed by the company's CEO is another criterion that candidates inquire about.

Diverse candidates are sensitive to the makeup of the interviewing team as well as the team's level of understanding and comfort in discussing the company's diversity initiative. Often, there are inquiries about the diversity makeup of top leadership, including the board of directors. They judge companies on their willingness and ability to capitalize on diverse markets here and abroad. They are more attracted to a company that has established a reputation as a good corporate citizen, one that supports using diverse suppliers to increase purchasing power and quality of life for the less privileged in the communities in which they serve.

Many multicultural candidates pay close attention to the rankings of *Fortune*, National Society of Black Engineers and *DiversityInc.com*, which bestow "best in class" awards to companies exemplifying excellence in recruitment of people of color and women. As a result, for many companies, their branding strategy now includes vying for and being included on elite annual lists of Best Companies to Work For. In fact, being cited on *just one* of the lists is no longer sufficient.

## Cost of Recruiting

According to *Business Week*, today it costs approximately $14,000 to hire a new grad engineer (not including relocation costs) and $100,000 to train him/her.[55]

One of the realities in this "new" economy, is that companies may be perennially understaffed. Making the right hiring decision, therefore, becomes even more crucial. According to Management Recruiters International, a search firm, it is estimated that hiring the wrong candidate for a managerial job can cost a company roughly three times that individual's salary.[56] Designing a sound strategy for recruiting diverse talent and including as many candidates as possible in that talent pool is critical.

*Vignette,* a software firm, for example, uses an acquisition strategy to gain talent by buying smaller companies that already sell the products or services it's seeking. *Cisco* is creating its own pipeline of talent by training and graduating more than 10,000 students globally from its virtual Networking Academy.

Even CEOs are beginning to participate in diversity recruitment, especially as they interface with their increasingly diverse customer base. I met a CEO of a Fortune 500 company recently on a plane. He shared with me how he got involved in diversity recruitment. He was meeting with his largest distributor, who just happens to be a woman. During the meeting, she chided him for not having a woman on his staff. Within three weeks, he hired a woman to head his Supply Chain Management organization.

Another leader with whom I served on a panel at a recent conference shared his first experience with diversity recruitment. He related that a manager of an investment firm, an African-American, that owns significant shares of his company, reminded the CEO that he had no people of color on his staff. That remark motivated the CEO to hire a person of color to manage his Procurement department. Such can be the result when bottom-line issues are at stake.

A well-defined and comprehensive diversity sourcing strategy will contribute to increasing the diversity representation of your company. Likewise, a process initiated for recruiting diverse talent can be used for all "hard-to-fill" positions. *Texas Instruments* recently revamped its diversity recruitment strategy and was selected by the Corporate Leadership Council as "best in class" for its efforts.[57]

It's the culture, behaviors and people systems that are important in recruitment. Companies must differentiate themselves as exemplary diversity employers where people choose to go, are made to feel welcome, thrive and ultimately, choose to stay. After all, it's harder to quit when you are contributing and feel valued. Let's look at some companies, which have demonstrated strength in recruiting diverse talent.

## Best Practices

Each year *DiversityInc.com* ranks the top ten companies for recruitment. As would be expected, the numbers, both in terms of employee representation as well as total hires in one year, tell the story. And it's not about how many people the company has hired into lower level jobs. *Fortune,* which also annually ranks companies on their commitment to diversity, states that in the average top-50 companies, people of color hold about 16% of the board seats, comprise 22% of officials and managers, and command 13% of the 50 largest paychecks. According to *Fortune,* those are indications that a company has gone beyond political correctness. After all, they state, "No company would fill its top slots with unqualified people just to look multicultural."[58]

*Pitney Bowes,* has designed an accountability system comprised of metrics that are tracked and reported directly to the CEO. *American Airlines* ties pay to diversity management, including recruitment and retention. *Eastman Kodak* has developed performance and behavior competencies for leaders that leverage diversity and create a culture of inclusion.

In 2001, *J.P. Morgan Chase* was cited by *DiversityInc.com* as the best company in America for diversity recruitment. 45% of total new hires in the previous year were people of color. These were not just new hires into entry-level jobs. 28% of managers hired were people of color with an equal percent being women managers. Their current workforce is 40% people of color.

*Proctor & Gamble* reported 34% of new hires were people of color in 2001. This excellent showing was largely the result of the acquisition of Clairol, another very diverse company. 25% and 29% of the their management are comprised of people of color and women, respectively. Proctor & Gamble is a company that utilizes its active employee resource groups (e.g., Asians, African-Americans, gays and lesbians, Latinos, people with disabilities and women) to leverage successful recruiting strategies.

Approximately 44% of new employees hired by *American Airlines* in 2001, were people of color. Almost 53% of managers are people of color with 42% women managers. American is recognized as a gay-friendly company, offering domestic partner benefits. It also tracks diversity management metrics, including hires and promotions, and ties managers' pay to achievement of goals.

*Verizon Communications* also made the top ten *DiversityInc.com* list of best diversity recruiting companies, belying the myth that technical companies cannot excel in this arena. Although it was not reported how many of the 2001 new hires were engineers, 37% were people of color. Of their management ranks, 23.5% and 45% were people of color and women respectively. Verizon also measures progress in hiring and promotions and offers a mentoring program for its employees.

With major lay-offs and restructuring having occurred in the recent past, there is a window of opportunity, like none we've seen in this country for some time, to hire excellent diverse talent.

In the war for talent, an organization's reputation for being inclusive is critical to its ability to recruit not only in the U.S., but from the rest of the world's rich talent base as well. It is even more crucial in retaining employees once they are hired.

## RETENTION

The second business competency that continues to be problematic for businesses is soaring turnover rates, even costlier to companies than making hiring errors. We are experiencing the end of company loyalty as we know it. With the GenXers (or Generation Xpensive, as some would have it) the attitude that work is nothing more than a "temporary assignment" is becoming more prevalent.

This also marks the end of the stigma that used to be attached to changing jobs. Once the economy rebounds, poaching employees will resume at a fevered pitch. Generous perks and signing bonuses will again become an expectation. As the McKinsey report states, the supply of tomorrow's executives is declining. Yet, they're much more opportunistic, mobile and likely to work for an estimated seven companies during their career, compared to three ten years ago.[59]

Knowing how to retain top people in such a challenging environment can be a real competitive advantage. Because diverse employees are in such high demand, programs that are developed and implemented to retain them can be used in overall retention efforts impacting all employees.

The ability to retain talent requires a continuous commitment to a culture that embraces and fosters uniqueness. Fundamental to a good retention strategy is the understanding that everyone needs to feel valued before they can strive for peak performance. Retention rates may increase as employees take pride in the efforts their leadership makes to increase diversity.

Of particular concern to most large companies is their general lack of success in retaining women, particularly those in leadership positions. According to a study by the Families & Work Institute, women managers were twice as likely as men to rate their career advancement opportunity as "fair" or "poor." Those that rated advancement opportunities low also tended to be less loyal, committed and satisfied on the job. Ultimately, women are twice as likely as men to leave.[60]

The key to effective retention is establishing a culture that is inclusive and promotes trust. Insecurity and mistrust drive turnover. Success requires commitment from the CEO and senior leadership that empowers employees to be as creative and productive as they can be. Communication that is open and consistent, both with employees and public constituencies such as customers, suppliers and shareholders, is key. Diversity needs to be as ingrained in a company's culture as customer satisfaction has become, where no one needs to be reminded of its necessity as processes and programs are designed and implemented.

Creating an inclusive culture is a challenge. Sustaining it over the long-term is even more difficult. A company needs to adopt a mindset of continuous learning and improvement in developing diversity skills (e.g., acquiring global intelligence and cultural competence), periodically evaluating metrics and accountability for effectiveness of skills training. Because people from different cultures tend to question why things are done the way they are, a company committed to diversity needs to demonstrate flexibility in policies and agility in revamping practices that have become antiquated. They also need to develop people systems that support diverse employees.

The key to effective diverse talent management is keeping employees once they're hired. If you can't, you'll be unable to respond to your customers. So, ask yourself the following questions:

- Do your diverse employees feel *included* in the day-to-day operations of your organization - on teams, in meetings or strategic-planning sessions, at after-work social events?

- Are they being properly *developed* and mentored? Is their potential to excel really being optimized?

- Are they being *promoted* into positions with increasing responsibility and visibility?

- Have your diverse employees been recipients of formal and informal recognition and *reward?*

- Are they smiling and having fun?

## Leadership Development and Accountability

Competencies and behaviors that support this commitment must be embraced and modeled by leaders and practiced at all levels of the organization. One of the selection criteria of future leaders should be their command of multicultural competencies and behaviors as well as their repertoire of diverse experiences domestically and depth of knowledge about cultures globally. Mastering different communication styles to meet the demands of any given situation is one such competency. Effective facilitation is another. Mentoring and being an active sponsor of women and people of color is crucial.

Employees who feel valued, are encouraged to perform to their potential, and are rewarded for doing so, are not as inclined to look for opportunities with the competition. Employees who see "people like them" in positions of power are more likely to remain with a company. They sense that the playing field really is level, and that there is opportunity for advancement.

Historically, line managers have not been held accountable for developing talent, much less diverse talent. That practice must change. If you treat people like they make a difference, they make a difference.

## Costs of Replacement

The estimates of what it costs to replace employees vary considerably. No one disputes the heavy financial toll that a "revolving door" syndrome places on organizations. Conservative estimates of replacing one experienced engineer range between $50,000 and $100,000. If that engineer is diverse, it will likely be more. More realistic estimates calculate replacement costs at *four times* the employee's annual salary. Multiply that figure by total turnover, and the costs are huge. John Challenger, CEO of Challenger, Gray & Christmas, an outplacement firm, estimates that one defection can cost as much as $100,000 when you consider lost productivity and replacement costs.[61] *Business Week* estimates costs to be a minimum of $112,000, when retraining costs are included.[62]

Companies need to be mindful of the impact downsizing and restructuring have on the diversity of an organization. It is during these times when there is sometimes a lapse in "management consciousness," quickly undoing years of work to create diversity in its ranks. Minority employees, often the last to be hired during booms, sometimes become the first fired when layoffs are conducted, especially when strict seniority rules prevail. The same is true during mergers and acquisitions. A company's ability to control attrition during unsettling times of change is crucial.

Incessant "brain-drain" causes production delays, diminished morale, loss of a corporate knowledge base and intellectual property, and retraining and replacement costs. Managers' time and attention is diverted from developing their existing employees to the time-consuming task of having to replace attrition.

High turnover interrupts product pipeline design and development. Customer service is interrupted, and maintaining that valued customer base is jeopardized.

If this situation persists and the manager's focus continues to be on hiring at the neglect of spending time with existing staff, those employees could begin their own job search. Two of the reasons most frequently cited in exit interviews for deciding to leave a company include lack of development opportunities and lack of a mentoring program. Develop people appropriately and promote aggressively, and much of the retention issues will vanish.

In a reactive mode of having to hire "warm bodies" as quickly as possible, less focus is placed on workforce planning and developing a skills acquisition sourcing strategy to meet future requirements. Such a strategy is critical to enhancing the capability of the organization down the road.

If a company stays the course and sustains an inclusive culture, it is more inclined to retain its talent base, subvert the "brain drain" and halt the supply stream of valued skills to the competition. It keeps innovation in its own house.

## Developing a Retention Strategy

According to the McKinsey study, a winning employee value proposition gives "life" to a culture and its values, and it instills *trust;* the key criterion to successful retention.[63] Also of importance is existing and continuous access to challenging work.

Essential components of a strategy that strengthens loyalty and allegiance to a company include:

* **People systems** (e.g., hiring, promotions, terminations, training, performance management, succession planning, compensation, etc.) need to be examined to determine how diversity-supportive they are. This includes unwritten rules that are so familiar to some, primarily Caucasian males, and unfamiliar to others, primarily people of color and women. Informal norms, that make or break you politically, based on doing things a certain way only because they've always been done that way (e.g., hiring in one's likeness) or limiting access to decision-making only to a select few (e.g., business being conducted on the golf course) need to cease. This is why a mentor is so important. He or she can explain the rules and can help a woman or person of color navigate the uncharted waters of the workplace.

* Enhanced **benefits** such as flexible work hours, telecommuting, on or near-site childcare, concierge services, domestic partner benefits and other work/life policies.

* **Career development** programs, including mentoring, coaching, skills training, career planning and other one-to-one relationships that include women and people of color.

- A "Key Talent" or **"high potential"** plan that identifies top performers, a succession plan and/or a "fast track" program, all three of which include women and people of color. (It is most important that you inform key talent of their value to the company and that they are slated for positions of greater responsibility. Not to do so risks their leaving).

With these programs, they can begin to contribute while they wait for a slot to open up. In *Winning the Talent War*, the author points out that the argument that "our industry is different, and it takes time to prepare people for a meaningful role in our company" no longer works in today's "short-attention-span environment."[64] It just leads to one staffing crisis after another. Other retention strategies include:

- Commitment to and support of affinity, or **employee resource groups,** participating to help achieve business goals, such as recruitment, retention and supplier procurement.

- **Accountability** and metric-imbedded scorecard tracking of diversity management reported on a quarterly basis.

- **Bonuses** tied to managing diverse talent in substantially the same ratio that Profit and Loss goals are rewarded. (Thirty-eight of *Fortune's* 50 Best Companies for Minorities to Work For, tie managers' bonuses to diversity goals.)[65]

- A **leadership** credo that adheres to the proposition, "hire hard and manage easy." Micromanagement and excessive bureaucratic requirements usually impede productivity and contribution.

- Frequent **recognition** that rewards ingenuity and top-notch performance.

- The fewer the rules and policies, the more **flexible** a company remains. Flexibility equates to nimbleness, ability to change and react quickly and maintain an open, receptive environment in order to take advantage of new market opportunities.

Women who work for supportive companies are typically more satisfied with their jobs, are sick less often, work later in their pregnancies and are more likely to return to their employer following childbirth. In a study done by the National Council of Jewish Women, 78% of women returned to work in accommodating companies, whereas only 32% returned to companies that were less obliging.

Several years ago, a company asked me to conduct a survey of women who had elected not to return to work following maternity leave. When asked what might have persuaded them to return, they overwhelmingly cited on-site childcare and flexible work hours. Having the ability to spend their lunch hour nursing their infant or taking their toddler to the cafeteria were very important factors in reducing stress.

Research conducted by the National Study of the Changing Workforce, found that working parents who experience fewer breakdowns in childcare arrangements are more satisfied with their work, less stressed and cope better than other parents. Telecommuting and non-traditional work arrangements are also important benefits that entice employees to stay with a company.[66]

## Best Practices

Out-of-the-box strategies like those implemented by *Ford, Delta, American, Avon* and *The New York Times* can have a positive impact on retention. All of these companies have provided computers and Internet access to their employees. This has the effect of encouraging employees to become computer literate as well as to continuously improve through learning, including acquiring cultural competence and global intelligence about their customers.

Another company which has "pushed the envelope" relative to its approach to effective retention is *Ernst and Young*. In a time when many companies are downsizing and severing relationships with employees, this accounting firm is doing the opposite. Ernst and Young has implemented a strategy of communicating the importance of life-long relationships between the company and its employees. Its Office of Workforce Retention reports that its focus has saved the company millions of dollars in recruitment costs, an otherwise significant drain on its bottom line.

One measure of a company's commitment to diversity is its support of employee resource groups. Sponsoring such groups positively impacts a company's ability to retain its diverse talent. There are a number of companies that have excelled in this arena.

I had the opportunity to benchmark the company that, in my opinion, has led all others in its historical and pro-active support of diversity, in general, and employee resource groups, in particular. When I asked *IBM* senior leadership which component of their diversity initiative most positively affected retention, they quickly responded the work of their employee resource groups. They also pointed out that employee resource groups have been instrumental in identifying new, diverse customers and applicants globally.

IBM has established a highly-functioning infrastructure to support diversity, with employee resource groups being at the heart of their strategy. IBM sponsors eight groups: Asians, African-Americans, Latinos, gays and lesbians, people with disabilities, Native Americans, women and men. (In fact, IBM is one of only a handful of companies successful in establishing a men's group, whose mission at IBM centers on resolving parenting issues for workers). In addition to being assigned its own senior leader as an advisor, each employee resource group has its own website, operating budget, network groups, diversity councils and task forces.

Another unique aspect of IBM's program is its global focus. Diversity task forces operate in all regions of the world. Since diversity does not carry the same meaning in many countries of the world that it does in the U.S., IBM has selected two issues to focus on that they have found to be common globally: increasing the number of women executives and addressing the issues of people with disabilities. IBM sponsors two-day Leadership Symposia for each of its employee resource groups every several years. Their highly touted Community Service Assignment Program, where they align with initiatives in their communities in need of assistance, also operates globally.

Philip Morris and Ford have demonstrated long-term commitment and sponsorship of employee resource groups. *Philip Morris* encourages its employees to interface with community groups - schools, churches and neighborhood associations. Employees state that having the ability to reach out and make a difference in their communities is a strong incentive for staying with Philip Morris. *Kraft Foods*, a member of Philip Morris' family of companies, is known for its work in tutoring and mentoring school-age children.

*Ford* has nine affinity groups. They play an important role in helping to test out product enhancements. Design engineers recently called upon several employee resource groups to corroborate Ford's intention of making the Windstar minivan family-friendly. This policy exemplifies implementation of a fundamental principle in diversity - valuing employees and empowering them to make suggestions about the products they make. Members of Ford's employee resource groups were key to gaining approval from senior leadership to extend employee benefits beyond family to include friends. This enabled friends of Ford employees to receive discounts on purchases of Fords, a win-win solution for them as well as the company.

Companies that have designed retention strategies often target diverse populations initially, since replacing them is often the most challenging and costly. Once implemented, retention strategies that prove effective with a targeted group are almost always effective for the overall workforce. According to *Fortune,* the following companies have achieved notable results in retention. Though not specifically stated, the assumption is that each of these companies incorporates a consideration for diversity in its process.

*General Electric* selects and grooms its future leaders from a slate of existing internal candidates, whose resumes are personally reviewed by the CEO. "Session C" is the process used to select attendees to the company's lauded and frequently benchmarked management training program. GE believes that giving top people the chance to develop within the company keeps them in the company.

*Home Depot*, which experiences a turnover rate that is estimated to be as much as 20% below the retail average, offers a stock purchase plan to employees, whom they refer to as "associates." This is a conscious effort on the part of the company to give status and opportunities for greater responsibility and compensation to its employees. Two years ago, only twelve of the company's 400 department heads came from the outside; the remainder were promoted from within. Higher management prides its reliance on the opinions and input of sales personnel, as opposed to district managers, feeling their sales force is closer to the customer.

*SAS Institute*, a software company, has experienced a turnover rate that is also enviable, approximately 4% compared to an industry average of 20%. According to a recent Harvard Business School study, that represents about a $50 million savings. A stable workforce also enables this company to produce product more cheaply and efficiently. Some of the benefits they offer that contribute to their low turnover rate include a low-cost day care facility; a cafeteria outfitted with high chairs so that employees can eat with their children; free access to a gym; a putting green and on-site massages.

*Cisco Systems* has acquired a reputation for integrating extremely well companies that they have acquired over the years. Mergers and acquisitions are risky business when it comes to retaining existing and acquired employees. Yet, Cisco has managed to acquire over 20 companies and has lost just 7% of the employees involved. To accomplish this, Cisco does due diligence up front and refuses to enter any kind of a business alliance if the culture, management practices or pay systems of the company to be acquired are not similar to their own. They learned early on that the most frequent reason cited for why mergers and acquisitions fail is due to incompatibility of cultures.

The People Department of *Southwest Airlines* spent over ten years analyzing the skills and behaviors of its employees as predictors of success. They then calibrated these criteria into questions to test candidates on the specific needs and requirements of each job as well as to the overriding attributes they wanted to perpetuate in their culture. The result has been a turnover rate of only 9%, lowest in the industry.[67]

Not only can diversity be leveraged to attract the best multicultural talent, it can also be harnessed to retain that talent. A challenge for businesses going forward will be to manage the generational clash of veterans, boomers, xers and nexters. Retaining older workers for their institutional knowledge and wisdom is smart business. There simply are not enough GenXers to fill the jobs of retiring older workers. Creating a strong coalition of the old and the new is a wise strategy.

## SUPPLIER PROCUREMENT

A large component of establishing a reputation as a good corporate citizen and a diversity employer of choice is creating opportunities for smaller businesses. In essence, a corporation gives back to the community, in which it resides, thereby creating purchasing power in these smaller entities.

It used to be that including efforts to do business with small suppliers or HUB (Historically Underutilized Business) businesses, exemplified a company's good will or "good faith" efforts in minority purchasing programs. Now, for companies with an appreciation for the changing demographics and their considerable purchasing power, it has become a *critical strategy* to tap into the emerging multicultural markets.

It's also a fiscally sound business practice. Companies can no longer exclude diversity suppliers from participating in their business and still expect them to buy their products. Diversity procurement is a pragmatic strategy that is in an enlightened company's self-interest. It's just common sense to have access to goods and services from the best and widest variety of suppliers.

Executing on this third business competency is a challenge, however. It is vital for companies that are serious about courting and maintaining relationships with diverse suppliers to create a strategy that commits them to setting and reaching diversity supplier goals. As well, they need to do a better job of providing suppliers access to information they need to bid on contracts. For large companies, this latter issue is often easier said than done. It's not uncommon for complaints to surface about the obstacles and bureaucracy that get in a supplier's way of trying to do business with a large company. Yet, once the process is defined, a diversity supplier procurement program is relatively easy to administer.

The opportunities lie in centralizing the effort within the company and capitalizing on economies of scale. The benefits to a company for implementing such a program are significant.

By the same token, it should be noted that not all small businesses are, in reality, large enough to do business with major corporations. The cut-off seems to be a small business with revenues of at least $15 million. Otherwise, managing the costs of doing business with large companies, such as conference calls, meetings, etc., can bury a smaller company. So can the risk of doing business with a corporation. Small companies need to have enough assets to insulate against breakdowns in the business relationship or occasional lawsuits.

## The Benefits

Companies no longer have an excuse for not forging relationships with businesses owned by women and people of color. In 1997, the most recent year for the data, women in the U.S. owned eight million businesses and people of color, three million. Women-owned businesses employ 15.5 million (all potential customers for Corporate America) and generate $1.4 trillion in revenues. Businesses owned by people of color employ 4.5 million and generate revenues of $600 billion.

These are staggering numbers that should provide a wake-up call to any company not trying to establish a business alliance with them. Corporate relationships with communities are strengthened through supplier diversity contracts. It goes without saying that companies with a diverse supplier base are more successful in gaining access to multicultural markets - customers that will purchase their goods and services.

Another advantage to a diversity supplier procurement program is the flexibility created when conducting business with a small supplier. They are usually able to react more quickly to critical issues. Often, the enterprising corporation realizes significant cost savings. Typically, these savings come via the lower cost-structure that small businesses have over larger suppliers. Many small diverse suppliers are often in proximity distance-wise to the company's customers. Many are recognized for having served niche markets for years. Other metrics that support the use of diverse suppliers include reduced time to market and just-in-time technical assistance.

Word travels fast amongst community-based diversity suppliers. A company that makes an effort to include diversity suppliers as a business strategy, receives favorable status in the communities in which it resides, and that carries over to the products it sells. A diversity procurement initiative further pushes a company's reputation as an employer of choice, attracting future workers to its ranks. A company that is involved in emerging-market communities, from diversity supplier initiatives to philanthropic activities, sends a strong signal of support to would-be customers and employees. In turn, the company is rewarded with gaining access to formerly untapped multicultural markets that would otherwise be impenetrable.

As Daryl Hodnett, group manager of Supplier Diversity Development for *Proctor & Gamble*, states:

> With minority populations ... quickly becoming the majority of the population tomorrow, we see a competitive advantage in increasing our business with entities

that reflect our country's diverse consumers. By doing business with diverse suppliers, we ... gain key insights into consumer behavior and preferences as a value-add to the quality services ... suppliers are already providing.[68]

With a slowdown in the economy and a need to "tighten belts," many companies have turned to outsourcing as a survival strategy, opening up even more opportunities to partner with women and minority-owned businesses. This was true of *Lucent Technologies*, where they estimate they saved $82 million in 2000, the difference between rates with traditional suppliers and diverse suppliers.

## Best Practices

According to *Minority Business News USA* and *Women's Enterprise* magazine, ten companies have hit the $1 billion mark for supplier diversity procurement, each of which has become an inaugural member of the publications' Billion-Dollar Roundtable in 2000. These illustrious companies include: *AT&T, Daimler Chrysler, Ford, General Motors, IBM, Lucent Technologies, Philip Morris, SBC Communications, Verizon* and *Walmart.*[69]

In addition, the Telecommunications Industry Association reports that companies in this sector spent almost $7.8 billion in 2000, roughly 12% of their $67 billion domestic-procurement budgets, with minority-owned, disabled veteran-owned and women-owned businesses. Seventy-four companies in this sector also signed the "Supplier Diversity Challenge" at SUPERCOMM, the telecom industry's largest annual convention, pledging to exceed $10 billion collectively in procurement with diversity suppliers.

As is the case for the other two business competencies, recruitment and retention, a company's commitment to diversity procurement is measured by the numbers. Many companies talk about making a commitment to allocating a certain percentage of their procurement budget to diverse suppliers but fail to follow through. A substantial commitment is considered to be 10% of that budget.

According to *DiversityInc.com, SBC Communications* was the biggest spender on diversity procurement in 2000 with 23% of its budget, about $3 billion, going to such suppliers. Its stated goal relative to internal demographics is not to mirror the civilian labor force, but rather to reflect the population that they serve. In California, SBC dominates the multicultural landscape in telecom services. By 2005, the ethnic market is expected to purchase $65 billion worth of services, the equivalent of half of today's market. Part of SBC's success in using diverse suppliers has been reduced delivery times to the customer base. They have achieved this by pairing small diverse suppliers to larger manufacturing entities. Having parts on demand has eliminated huge warehouse costs. As Stephen Welch, President of Procurement for SBC, has stated:

> As our industry became more competitive, we saw we could get good business solutions from small businesses. We also knew that the demographics of our customer base were changing, and that minority communities were among our best customers.[70]

*Ford*, recognized by many in Corporate America as having the premier diversity procurement program, spent the largest dollar amount on diverse suppliers, just edging out SBC Communications, with $3.5 billion of its $90 billion procurement budget being used with over 400 diversity suppliers. Ford has also instituted a "first-tier" program, whereby they request all of their primary suppliers to buy at least 5% of all the goods and services they use from diversity-owned small businesses, or risk a continued relationship with Ford. According to Ford, this thrust now generates approximately $1 billion in minority purchasing by first-tier suppliers. As Dr. Renaldo Jensen, Director of Supplier Diversity at Ford states:

> If supplier diversity doesn't result in wealth, training or quality-of-life improvements in the minority community that you're servicing, then you're missing the boat. If you are not creating wealth in the same communities where you are selling your products by creating small business development, then you are not doing your job.[71]

*IBM* was preaching the values of doing business with an increasingly diverse customer and supplier base years before other industries became enlightened. They have remained steadfast and consistent in their commitment in this area. Last year IBM spent almost 13% of its procurement budget, of roughly $1.5 billion, on diversity suppliers.

*Philip Morris,* including Kraft Foods, Miller Brewing Company and Philip Morris U.S.A., sets aggressive records in diversity supplier procurement. According to *DiversityInc.com,* there appears to be considerable support and requirements for accountability from its CEO, Geoffrey Bible. While there is no stated percentage goal for diverse suppliers, the Philip Morris family of companies spent $1.4 billion last year on diversity procurement, 8% of its total budget. Kraft Foods has been cited as one of the country's most tenacious practitioners of diversity procurement.

## CHALLENGES AND OPPORTUNITES

From the previous Business Imperatives, we know that manual work will continue to be replaced in the future by knowledge work. There will also continue to be a skills shortage to fill jobs, particularly in technical fields, both in the U.S. and the expanding global economy. As a company prepares to come to terms with an increasingly diverse workforce, there are some issues that it should address:

• Examine people systems, behaviors, leadership styles and cultural norms to ensure the company is poised to attract, develop and retain a *world-class* workforce. Make certain that practices support diversity, rather than subvert it. Build consideration for diversity into a policy *before* implementing it, not as an after thought. For example, require that diversity consciousness be reflected in all training classes, not just those dealing with diversity.

• Re-examine policies regarding religious diversity in the workplace. Currently, there are more Moslems in the U.S. than Jews, Episcopalians or Presbyterians. Issues such as different diets, different attire and work schedules will need to be addressed.

• Recruiting needs to be strategic and incorporated in workforce planning. Ignoring the predictions of a labor shortage will perpetuate conducting recruitment in a reactive mode, hardly a condition in which to win a war for talent. There is little downside to workforce planning.

• Design creative recruiting strategies to attract multicultural workers, particularly older workers, where the largest growth will occur. This may require offering non-traditional work arrangements and proactive benefits packages, such as expanded health insurance coverage for elders, including long-term care. Many workers will have longer living parents, making elder benefits attractive. Other non-traditional sources of labor need to be explored (see Appendix V) and work/life balance programs researched for possible implementation.

- Survey employees to find out why they are leaving. Do so at the right time in a manner that elicits honest feedback. Turnover rarely shows up on the balance sheet, yet its costs can be insidious. Managers need to be held accountable for retention. As long as voluntary turnover is viewed as a human resources issue that is solved by filling vacant positions, the problem will only be exacerbated. HR and management end up spending more time on recruitment rather than retention, where the effort needs to be focused.

- If involuntary turnover is high, you need to examine your hiring process. Obviously, the wrong people are being hired, and the costs of recruiting are not being contained.

- Develop relationships with and create wealth in small diverse businesses in the communities in which you operate in the U. S. and globally. Establish goals to increase procurement spending with diverse suppliers and measure for results. This is necessary in order to integrate supplier diversity efforts in overall business practices.

## CONCLUSION

We live in a business environment with an increasingly diverse customer base and workforce. A critical shortage of skilled labor, particularly technical talent, for whom the competition is fierce, both here and abroad, presents a sense of urgency.

With this challenge comes opportunity for a company to thrive and excel. It will require due diligence on a company's part in training leaders and the existing workforce in global intelligence and cultural competence. It will require, in some cases, a cultural make-over to create a powerful organizational fabric, comprised of vision, values and systems, that intertwine synergistically and reflect trust, respect and a belief in the inclusion of all people, particularly people of difference.

Only with this foundation will companies be able to attract and retain employees, shareholders, customers, business partners and suppliers. Only then will they be able to improve on three of their most important internal business competencies, *recruitment, retention and supplier procurement*, and perform for success and competitive advantage. Companies have already learned that not executing these competencies well is very costly – to the bottom line and to their reputation. As the McKinsey Report states, "Talent matters. It probably matters more than tangible assets such as financial capital or physical plants, or even intangibles like brand and market position."[72]

## SUMMARY HIGHLIGHTS
# Business Imperative 5: Need for Better Business Competencies

- A commitment to and excellence in executing a diversity recruiting strategy is no longer optional for companies that want to compete successfully for talent.

- Job seekers, including non-diverse candidates, prefer to work for a company with a demonstrated commitment to diversity.

- If supplying the pipeline is neglected, creating diversity at higher levels in the organization down the road will be much more challenging.

- A company's commitment to an inclusive culture is crucial. So is the institutionalization of systems that promote development and opportunity for all employees.

- The branding strategy of many companies now includes vying for placement on elite annual lists of Best Companies to Work For.

- Fundamental to a good retention strategy is the understanding that everyone needs to feel valued before they can strive for peak performance.

- The key to effective retention is establishing a culture that is inclusive and promotes trust. Insecurity and mistrust drive turnover.

- Replacement costs four times the employee's annual salary. Multiply that figure by total turnover, and the costs are huge.

- Incessant "brain-drain" causes production delays, diminished morale, loss of a corporate knowledge base and intellectual property, and retraining costs.

- Managers' time and attention is diverted from developing their existing employees to the time-consuming task of having to replace attrition.

- A mentor is important in explaining the unwritten rules and helping a woman or person of color navigate the uncharted waters of the workplace.

- Not only can diversity be leveraged to attract the best multicultural talent, it can also be harnessed to retain that talent.

- A challenge for businesses going forward will be to manage the generational clash of veterans, boomers, xers and nexters.

- There are not enough GenXers to replace retiring boomers. Retaining older workers for their institutional knowledge and wisdom is smart business.

- Companies can no longer exclude diversity suppliers from participating in their business and still expect them to buy their products.

- The opportunities lie in centralizing the diversity procurement effort to capitalize on economies of scale and track results. The benefits to a company for implementing such a program are significant.

# BUSINESS IMPERATIVE #6:

# ENHANCED CREATIVITY

We must become a model of inclusion around the world. We need creative talents, the enthusiastic commitment, the ideas and contribution of every HP employee. Invention requires creativity; creativity requires true diversity.

The value proposition for diversity is very clear:
- Diversity drives creativity
- Creativity drives invention
- Invention drives profitability and business success.[73]

> - Carly Fiorina, CEO,
> Hewlett-Packard

## INCLUSION

When an organization creates a culture of inclusion, its ability to out-recruit and out-retain the competition is optimized. The more diversity of experiences, backgrounds, lifestyles and perspectives that is cultivated in an organization, the greater array and richness of ideas. A culture needs to be adaptive. The one-size-fits-all monolithic culture of the past can no longer work. As Dr. Krishna Athreya of Iowa State University in her testimony before the Commission on the Advancement of Women and Minorities in Science, Engineering and Technology Development (CAWMSET) stated several years ago:

> A safe and equitable learning ...workplace is one where creativity is recognized and promoted (even, or especially, when it leads to non-standard results). Creativity is a critical element for SET advancement. Diversity fosters creativity.[74]

And at the Digital Connections Conference in San Jose in May of 2000, Carly Fiorina, CEO of **HP**, remarked:

> Diversity nourishes the soul of our company - and truly great companies have souls. Diversity fills critical roles in our organizations. Diversity inspires creativity and inventiveness. And inventiveness and creativity are core virtues of this new economy...It's up to all of us to create an environment that embraces diversity...rather than one that simply accommodates it.[75]

Conversely, a culture that is insensitive to differences, thereby excluding participation and contribution of certain individuals and shutting them down - or out, limits the potential of organizations to create products and services that are expected by the customer.

## HOMOGENEITY vs. HETEROGENEITY

Companies with a high degree of conformity are not easy places to join if you're a person of difference. Conformity is not an enabler of creativity and innovation. It is the great gatekeeper of the status quo. Homogeneous cultures foster one point of view. "Groupthink" reigns as different opinions and solutions are discouraged. Opportunities for increases in breakthrough technology, innovative products and patentable processes are missed. The less inclusive and homogeneous a culture tends to be, the more that creativity, and, in turn, productivity, get stifled. You may have fewer arguments in a homogeneous group, but you'll likely get uninspiring answers.

There is research to support the argument that diversity generally enhances creative, problem-solving capability. In 1972, social psychologist, Irving Janis, studied the dynamics of a number of poor decisions regarding national security, including such events as Pearl Harbor and the Bay of Pigs. He concluded that all these decisions suffered from "groupthink," which occurs when homogeneous teams stifle criticism, questioning and differing opinions in favor of maintaining group cohesion - all with tragic costs.[76]

- In a landmark study, Margaret Neale from the University of California at Berkeley, found that, while greater diversity on teams produced more conflict; it also led to more idea generation. She concluded that while it may take longer for diverse teams to gel, the quality and creativity of the results can be much higher.[77]

- In 1991, Cox and Blake found in one of their studies that a heterogeneous team in its formative stage needs guidance and balance amongst its members. "Decision quality is best when neither excessive diversity nor excessive homogeneity are present." It is helpful that team members share common "values and norms" to promote problem-solving and innovation. The organization, in turn, must provide a cohesive and unified goal in support of the team in order to achieve competitive advantage.[78]

- Research conducted by Watson, Kumar and Michaelsen in 1993, found while diversity initially slowed down newly-formed teams, in the long term, heterogeneous teams actually scored "significantly higher on range of perspectives and alternatives generated."[79]

- In a study done in 2000 by the American Council on Education on the effects of diversity in the college classroom, it was found that the presence of racial and ethnic diversity helped students to better achieve their learning goals. According to students and faculty, a wider range of experiences present in a heterogeneous classroom enhanced the curriculum and generated more complex thinking than one that was homogeneous. Students stated that conflict and tension actually catalyzed learning not only about others, but about themselves as well. Exposure to other ideas and viewpoints caused awareness in the students about their own biases. Faculty reported that multi-racial/ ethnic classes had a positive effect on students' cognitive and personal development because it "challenges stereotypes, broadens perspectives and sharpens critical thinking."[80]

• In her seminal work, *The Change Masters*, Rosabeth Moss Kanter found that one of the most important criteria for team success is differences in perspective and assumptions. She also found that the more creative companies deliberately established heterogeneous teams in order to "create a marketplace of ideas, recognizing that a multiplicity of points of view needs to be brought to bear on a problem." These companies had done a better job than most in eradicating racism and sexism. They were also more financially successful.[81]

## Fugio Masuoka's Story

A good example of the effects of a strongly homogeneous culture is the story of Fugio Masuoka. Employed by Toshiba, he invented flash memory, a technology used in semiconductors. For this he was awarded the Institute of Electrical & Electronics Engineers' Morris N. Liebman Memorial Award. In 2001 flash memory had sales of $76 billion. These chips went into products worth more than $3 trillion, including computers, automobiles and mobile phones. Flash memory was the most important semiconductor innovation of the 1990s; it should have made Masuoka very rich.

However, Masuoka lives in Japan, and his employer recognized his efforts by awarding him a bonus worth only "a few hundred dollars." Masuoka claims that Toshiba then tried to move him from his senior post to a position where he could do no further research. What's worse, the company failed to capitalize on its initial technology lead and let rival Intel take control of his invention and the eager market.

Masouka's tale illustrates how Japan lost the semiconductor race with the U.S., which it controlled in the 1980s. This was due, in part, by neglecting basic research in favor of applied work on established products. It was also due to Toshiba's failure to realize that, in the semiconductor business, an organization needs to be highly innovative. Also at play was the high context cultural trait that is characteristic of Japan, which favors team recognition over individual achievement.

Lack of tolerance and recognition for innovative thinking in Masouka's case stifled creativity and contributed to a missed opportunity of continued technological leadership and increased revenues. As a postscript, Masuoka is now working on an even more important invention, a "three-dimensional silicon-based semiconductor," which will increase the capacity of semiconductors by a factor of ten. This time he is applying in the U.S. for patents in his own name and is seeking venture-capital funding so that he can reap the rewards of his creativity in a manner more in tune with the U.S., than Japan.[82]

## The Benefits of Heterogeneity

Breakthroughs come when "either/or" thinking is replaced with "both/and," blending sometimes seemingly incongruous perspectives into one rich and innovative solution.

Heterogeneous cultures consciously widen the bandwidth of desired differences, creating the broadest possible resource base with 360-degree vision and capabilities to meet the requirements of potential scenarios. With a larger portfolio of skills and ideas, an organization based on inclusion is better suited to respond quickly and innovatively to the demands of the diverse market. The usability of a product can be broadened to meet the needs of an expanded customer base.

One measure of creativity is patents. In the U. S. the three most populous and diverse states, California, New York and Texas also lead the country in numbers of patents, correlating exactly with their percentage of diversity. In fact, the U.S., the most diverse country in the world, accounted for 56% of all patents in 1999, the most recent year of record.

Heterogeneity in problem-solving produces better decisions through a wider range of perspectives and critical analysis of different issues. Team members from the same backgrounds generally have a narrower range of experiences. By including more diversity of ideas and experiences (non-mainstream in nature) on the team, the possibilities of getting a broader range of ideas and solutions is enhanced. The overall quality of the decisions is likely to improve as consensus of opinion develops and the number of times that decisions need to be revisited decreases.

This argument rings true for companies doing business globally, where diversity means not just ethnicities, but nationalities, as well. As a recent *Fortune* article noted, "a group with eight passports represented will be stronger than a group with one or two."[83]

Assuming they come from a culture that has encouraged speaking up, people from diverse backgrounds and experiences often challenge the status quo, including business practices and processes. (A commitment to an inclusive culture will support healthy debate and encourage more reticent employees to speak up). As "outsiders" and people who see and think differently, they wonder why things are done a certain way as opposed to another - a way that seems more natural to them. If managed properly, this mindset can be very healthy to a company, preventing it from continuing antiquated practices, keeping it nimble and flexible with a bent toward continuous improvement.

This role of questioning is also often played by someone new to the organization, particularly someone from another industry (also a component of diversity). All too often, companies pay lip service to diversity while the "not-invented-here" syndrome and "corporate training," both of which instill conformity, flourish. These practices stultify creativity and diversity of thought, the component of diversity that counts most in a thriving organization.

Until a culture is established that values differing perspectives and experiences and is inclusive of diversity of thought, will employees begin to trust the organization enough to take risks and offer ideas that break traditional rules. This is a fundamental requirement for wealth creation, both for the company and the individual.

Many companies talk about "intrapreneurship," giving people permission to take risks; but the rewards are generally minimal for those who succeed. And, if they fail, they generally get fired. In a truly inclusive environment, no one really cares how old you are, where you grew up, what academic degrees you've earned, where you've worked or what style clothes you wear. What counts is the quality of thinking, the competence, the power of vision and the courage to ask "why?"

## THE COSMOPOLITAN COMPANY

"Mighty is the mongrel," proclaims Pascal Zachary in a stimulating article in the July 2000 issue of *Fast Company*. The mixing of races and ethnicities is at a record level globally, he states. It presents us with a new business model: "mixing minimizes isolation ... spawns creativity, nourishes the human spirit, spurs economic growth, empowers nations." Going mongrel, or becoming heterogeneous, is not only right and good, according to the author; it is the antidote to stagnation and a continuing replenishment of innovation and creativity.

The conditions for creating wealth have changed in support of diversity. Those companies wishing to profit from the changing economic conditions must view this "mongrelization" as their best option. As previously mentioned, the most creative people are those who tend to question accepted views and consider conjectural ones, a trait that diversity contributes. "Divergent thinking is an essential ingredient of creativity. Diverse groups produce diverse thinking. Ergo, diversity promotes creativity." Innovation no longer relies on "platoons of similar people," according to Zachary.

The new economy calls for a cosmopolitan corporation, where employees are encouraged to retain their differences in order to capitalize on their uniqueness and the inherent creative tension. Cosmopolitan companies are not merely tolerant of differences, they ask employees to revel in them. They don't rely on internal referrals; they seek out strangers. "By pouring their authentic identities into their jobs, employees become more creative and effective," Zachary alleges. Cosmopolitan companies reject the traditional dominant style in favor of a kaleidoscope of styles to promote creativity. People grow and are more creative when they interact with a critical mass of strangers, preferably in more than one place.[84]

The German pharmaceuticals company, *Schering AG*, is a good example of a company reinventing and transforming itself to this new model. Traditionally, recruiting in Europe has been limited by country boundaries, minimizing the possibility of mixing or fostering diversity. Schering's new recruiting strategy is to hire the best people, regardless of their nationality. As would be expected, there is resistance from within Schering, and it remains to be seen whether this new model can be implemented. But the seed has been planted.

The inherent advantage to the U.S. is that we have had more mongrels than anyone else. As a result, we stand to get a "bigger bang" from our diversity than anyone else.

## THE IMPORTANCE OF DIVERSITY IN ENGINEERING

One's creativity is bounded by one's experience. Fundamentally, men, women, people of color, people with disabilities, gays, the older and the younger see and experience the world in a different way. These differences are the "DNA pool" from which creativity springs. As William Wulf, President of the National Academy of Engineering, so powerfully and eloquently states:

> Every time an engineering problem is approached with a pale male design team, it may be difficult to find the best solution, understand the design options, or know how to evaluate the constraints.

> [Though] …not the way it is usually described, … I believe that engineering is profoundly creative … In any creative profession, what comes out is a function of the life experiences of the people who do it … [Without] diversity, we limit the set of life experiences that are applied, and as a result, we pay an opportunity cost – a cost in products not built, in designs not considered, in constraints not understood, in processes not invented … We may not even understand the full dimension of the problem. Our profession is diminished and impoverished by a lack of diversity.[85]

Engineering designs must reflect the culture (and taboos) of multicultural consumers in a global economy. Without diversity, these sensitivities may not be reflected, and product will not sell. Even worse, the range of design options considered in a team without diversity will be smaller, and the desired product may never be developed.

Dr. Wulf continues, "It's that the constraints on the design will not be properly interpreted. It's that the product that serves a broader international customer base, or a segment of this nation's melting pot, or our handicapped, may not be found."[86] It is that the most "elegant" solution may never be discovered. While the costs may not be economic in nature, there is an opportunity cost – design options not pursued, customer needs unfulfilled, "might-have-beens" lost and buried.

On the need to improve the image of engineering, a cause Dr. Wulf personally champions, he cites a poll conducted by the American Association of Engineering Societies. This study found that only 2% of the public associated the word "invent" with engineering; only 3% associated the word "creative" with engineering. However, 5% associated "train operator" with engineer!

Such a misunderstanding of what an engineer does is profoundly disturbing. The public has seen engineering's analytical side and not the creative side, but they also see engineers finding flaws in their creativity, rather than celebrating it. Only when the image of engineers is elevated and their roles better understood will enrollment in engineering improve for women and people of color. This declining enrollment trend exists in spite of the fact that starting salaries for new engineering graduates are averaging $40,000 or more. Dr. Wulf continues:

> We need to understand why in a society so dependent on technology, a society that benefits so richly from the results of engineering, a society that rewards engineers so well, engineering isn't perceived as a desirable occupation.

> The central problem ... is our dull image, an incorrect image, an image that ignores the existential joys of engineering ... By failing to attract a diverse engineering workforce, we diminish what engineering can contribute to society, and society pays an opportunity cost.[87]

## CHALLENGES AND OPPORTUNITIES

Creative people are often criticized for being both conservative and rebellious at the same time, often to the disgruntlement of management. The question is, which benefits the company more in the long-term: creativity or fitting in? Often, the freshest ideas come in the heat of debate. One challenge for corporations will be to not only increase their comfort level with healthy debate and dialogue but to welcome them as new rules of engagement for doing business. Challenging the status quo is a desirable behavior in an inclusive culture.

Without diversity on teams and teams being empowered, creativity will languish. However, managing diverse teams is challenging even for the most skilled leader. Managing diverse teams on a global scale is even more so. It requires a specially trained leader who is culturally competent and not "culture-bound", vigilant in macromanaging without stifling creativity, and capable of communicating goals effectively to a multicultural group.

## CONCLUSION

Diversity is not just "the right thing to do." It's a competitive advantage. Diversity of perspectives and less conformity to norms leads to more creative products and processes. The practice of ongoing, continuous intercultural learning that occurs when new cultural situations are encountered and reacted to produces growth and understanding, not only in one's work, but in one's personal life as well.

A culture must continuously offer great talent new opportunities for creative achievement - or they will go elsewhere. An inclusive culture does not tolerate a management mindset that touts ownership of people. Managers can't hold onto talent who want to try new things but are not supported.

SUMMARY HIGHLIGHTS
# Business Imperative 6: Enhanced Creativity

- Conformity is not an enabler of creativity and innovation. It is the great gate-keeper of the status quo.

- Homogeneous cultures foster one point of view. "Groupthink" reigns as different opinions and solutions are discouraged.

- Heterogeneous cultures consciously widen the bandwidth of desired differences, creating the broadest possible resource base with 360-degree vision and capabilities to meet the requirements of potential scenarios.

- With a larger portfolio of skills and ideas, an organization based on inclusion is better suited to respond quickly and innovatively to the demands of the diverse market.

- Heterogeneity in problem-solving produces better decisions through a wider range of perspectives and critical analysis of different issues.

- In a truly inclusive environment, no one really cares how old you are, where you grew up, what academic degrees you've earned, where you've worked or what style clothes you wear. What counts is the quality of thinking, the competence, the power of vision and the courage to ask "why?"

- Differences are the "DNA pool" from which creativity springs.

# BUSINESS IMPERATIVE #7:

# IMPROVED
# PRODUCTIVITY

When the five-year, 11-year and 20-year financial performance of companies engaged in diversity ... is compared to the performance of those that are not doing such work or are doing it poorly, the former companies significantly outperform the latter in terms of sales, growth, profit growth and performance in a downturning economy.[88]

- V. Robert Hayles
   Diversity in Corporate America

## THE IMPACT OF EMPLOYEE PERCEPTION ON PRODUCTIVITY

In an inclusive environment, the top priority is to optimize the potential of every employee through continuous skill acquisition and increasing levels of responsibility. This in turn leads to greater productivity.

Typically, people who understand one another collaborate better. The efficiency of their communication improves. They are more able to deal constructively with interpersonal conflict and learn from it. Working through diversity issues is excellent preparation for continuous learning, the ability to change, and innovation, three of the most important core values for most corporations today.

Research has been conducted to support the correlation between diversity and increased productivity. Ann Morrison led a team studying 16 organizations they considered to be role models in their implementation of diversity programs. Their conclusions were:

> To the extent that diversity efforts can alleviate the problems and improve the perceptions of employees - both the non-traditional employees who have borne the brunt of discriminatory treatment in many organizations and their white male counterparts, who must also be prepared and motivated to perform - productivity will be improved.[89]

In 1990, Robert Eisenberger and his colleagues found a positive relationship between employees' perceptions of being valued and included and their attendance and job performance.[90] Previous research conducted in two separate studies by Birnbaum and Ziller showed that heterogeneous groups were more productive than homogeneous groups.[91]

Simply put, employees who are happy at work are at work more often. More time at work produces more work, which translates into more products and services generated and lower costs per unit, leading to greater profits.

If diversity does indeed positively impact organizational productivity, we should be able to point to competitive advantage. Ann Morrison and her team did draw a strong correlation between the companies they studied, all of which had model diversity programs, and the *Fortune* list of "most admired" companies. "Most admired" included, among others, these criteria: quality management, quality of goods and services, innovation, financial soundness and ability to attract and retain top talent. Over 80% of the companies Morrison studied placed in the top 20% of *Fortune's* list. More than 70% ranked in the top half within their own industry.

## FACTORS THAT UNDERMINE PRODUCTIVITY

There are numerous factors that prevent productivity from being optimized in an organization. The most significant are conflict, underutilization of employees and disempowerment.

### Conflict

Conflict occurs at work due to personality clashes, differing opinions and cultural misunderstanding. Obviously, when someone is engaged in conflict, their energy and focus is distracted from work, and productivity decreases. It is estimated that 35% of management's time is spent on conflict resolution, which decreases their productivity by pulling them away from their major responsibilities of growing the business and their employees.

### Underutilization

Inclusion in a company's culture creates more trust, more authenticity, more risk-taking and a playing-to-win attitude. When people feel welcome, they perform, create and innovate better. Perception of opportunity improves loyalty, engagement and performance. When employees feel disregarded, productivity and quality may be compromised and ROI lost. Absenteeism, turnover, recruiting and retraining costs run rampant. Customer deadlines are missed. Innovation declines. The following dichotomy can be drawn to illustrate the impact underutilization has on the bottom line:

| **Utilized** | **Underutilized** |
| --- | --- |
| Loyalty | Turnover |
| Reliable Performance | Absenteeism/Missed Deadlines |
| Affiliation/Perception of Being Valued | Low Morale/Dissatisfaction |

Innovation/Risk Taking . . . . . . . . . . . . . . . . . . Disengaged/Resistance
Productivity . . . . . . . . . . . . . . . . . . . . . . . . . . . Poor Quality/Rework
ROI    . . . . . . . . . . . . . . . . . . . . . . . . . . . . Replacement/Retraining

Time is wasted with conflicts and misunderstandings. Conflict in the workplace can distract, de-energize and derail employees from being fully engaged and productive.

Greater productivity can be expected from employees who get along, enjoy their work and believe they can be successful. When morale and performance are high, and people feel fully utilized; organizational productivity improves. While the cost of changing an organization's culture to one of inclusion can be significant, the payback is often increased productivity and return-on-investment that can offset the costs of a diversity initiative.

Another way to quantify the undermining effects of underutilization is to position diversity strategies in such a way that productivity is enhanced. For example, research was conducted in 1987 by Chusmir and Durand. They showed that a 12% productivity gain could be achieved by reducing some existing barriers for women that prevented their full utilization, such as offering flex time and emergency care for sick children. If those women comprise half of the workforce, then the result would be a 5% productivity gain overall for the company.[92]

Bill Guillory, a diversity consultant and author, estimates the underutilization of women and people of color to be on the average approximately 70% and 65% of capacity, respectively. He documents these findings through numerous surveys he's done with many of his clients as well as studies from various business schools. This loss of productivity obviously impacts the bottom line in significant ways. He illustrates with the following examples:

> An organization employing 15,000 women earning an average annual income of $25,000, producing at an average of 70% of their capacity, results in $113 million loss in annual revenue.

Likewise, a corresponding calculation for 9,000 minorities earning an average annual income of $25,000, producing at an average of 65% of their capacity, results in loss of $79 million a year.[93]

Making similar extrapolations for your company will underscore the correlation between managing diversity effectively and the bottom line.

## Disempowerment

Empowerment expands the capacity of an individual to perform at optimal levels. A culture that is committed to attracting, respecting, including and fully utilizing people of difference creates trust and a passion for authenticity and uniqueness that unleashes this capacity to perform to one's fullest extent. Diversity and empowerment go hand-in-hand in enabling creativity and productivity. Organizational dysfunction occurs when one or the other is missing.

What are the factors in a workplace that disempower people? Mostly, it's those everyday acts of exclusion, devaluation and discouragement that push people of difference down - or out. It's what *Business Week* has termed "micro-inequities." Seen as a single event, they may appear to be benign or trivial. Viewed systematically, they are cultural norms that can ruin careers and company productivity.

Some micro-inequities are so woven into the culture, they appear, if discerned at all, to be unbiased. They can reside in company norms, like preference for "face time" and nine-hour-work days, rather than more appropriate metrics such as productivity and quality. Certainly, the latter expectations better serve a working parent, for example, who works half days or from a virtual office.

These cultural norms can be embedded in seemingly unbiased staffing practices. Cursory interviews and decisions made on first-impressions, often based on the candidate's similarity to the interviewer (e.g., the "halo effect") is one example. These norms can go unchallenged for the sake of expediency and filling that requisition quickly with a warm body or because "it's always been done that way."

The fact that someone has an accent can unconsciously translate to an assumption that the person is not competent in making an effective presentation or in understanding directions. A colleague of mine from Egypt, a department manager of a critical engineering project, shared with me that he was denied the opportunity to present his team's research to the CEO because his boss felt his accent would detract from the quality of the presentation.

While blatant, intentional discrimination has mostly been eliminated from the workplace, forms of highly subtle discrimination remain. These are the inadvertent actions often committed by "unconsciously incompetent" individuals, arising from unspoken and subliminal assumptions.

One of my Japanese colleagues, who works for a major U.S. firm, told me that she was denied a promotion to a leadership position by her manager because he felt she lacked leadership skill. This assessment was not based on her abilities and performance (she had received "outstanding" ratings on her last four reviews). Instead it was based on his observation that she was too quiet, aloof and disinterested during team meetings and, therefore, would not make a good leader. What he failed to take into account was that, given her cultural background, she believed that challenging another team member's idea was tantamount to assassinating his character. In the Japanese culture, consensus and face-saving are more important than being right. When she offered ideas, her suggestions were not acknowledged. Yet, a few moments later, when a male co-worker came up with the same idea, he received recognition. In an inclusive environment, that manager would be demonstrating a skill fundamental to effective diversity leadership - ensuring that all participants in a meeting are engaged and heard.

Following are examples of common micro-inequities that can be found in the workplace:

## Micro-Inequities in the Workplace

Halo Effect . . . . . . . . . . . . . . . . . . . . . . . . . . Meeting Dynamics/Etiquette
Insistence on Face Time . . . . . . . . . . Expedient/Closed Selection Decisions
Assumptions . . . . . . . . . . . . . . . . . . . . . . . . Lack of Cultural Knowledge
Racial Slurs/Jokes . . . . . . . . . . Intolerance of Accents/Language Difficulties
Stereotyping . . . . . . . . . . . . . . . . . . . . . . . . . . . Reduced Expectations
Token Assignments . . . . . . . . . . . . . . . . . . . . . . . . . . . . . . Retaliation

Other micro-inequities prevail in the workplace. A landmark study by Catalyst, the prestigious organization dedicated to the advancement of women, found that 65% of women of color in management left their jobs due to employers failing to address subtle gender bias.[94] Another benchmark study in 1995 by the Center for Creative Leadership found what subsequent research persists in reporting - people continue to be disempowered by managers' greater comfort in dealing with "people like them."[95]

Columbia School of Business and Korn/Ferry International, a search firm, conducted a study that found that 45% of minority executives stated they had been the target of a racial or cultural joke at work.[96] This figure does not include the unwitting acts of insensitivity that occur in the workplace fairly regularly.

One of my openly gay colleagues shared with me how frequently he hears jokes about sexual orientation in the cafeteria, in the restroom, even in meetings. Another former co-worker, who is a lesbian and in the closet, goes to great lengths to hide her sexual orientation, fearing retaliation. She has pictures in her office of a male cousin, whom she passes off to cube mates as her significant other. To gain acceptance by her heterosexual colleagues she fabricates stories about her social activities. On the rare occasions that she attends after-hours work functions, she brings her cousin. Since she can't challenge them, she endures insensitive comments about sexual orientation made by her co-workers.

Such micro-inequities affect motivation, concentration, stress and other health factors that detract from overall productivity. They also impact a company's retention.

Earl G. Graves, the founder of *Black Enterprise,* recalls inviting some businessmen to a charity dinner his magazine was sponsoring. Before accepting, some who received invitations needed to know whether there would be other white people at the table.[97] Whites carry an expectation, unconscious to be sure, that the world will be accommodating to them. The prospect of not being in the majority is often intimidating.

Similarly, it is often difficult for whites to understand what it's like on a sales call to be pegged as the "junior colleague" simply because one's skin happens to be black. We are reminded when we pick up the newspaper or watch the news of examples of "conscious," less subtle, assumptions about people of color that, when taken to the extreme, become pernicious forms of discrimination. We call it racial profiling – disempowerment in its most heinous form.

Nearly 60% of minority executives say they've observed a double standard in how assignments, especially meaningful assignments with profit & loss responsibility, are doled out. Often minority managers are held to lower expectations or pigeonholed in dead-end assignments. They are frequently held back because no white manager will "take a chance" on handing them that first substantive assignment. David A. Thomas of Harvard Business School says minority managers spend more time in the "bullpen" waiting for their chance. Once they get that first plum assignment, often they have to prove themselves yet again.

"We see people of color incurring a tax, even when they are superior per-formers," Thomas says. This subtle discrimination - the disempowerment - continues as they are left out of high-profile assignments, deprived of the opportunity to exhibit skills needed to earn promotions. Thomas' research supports the widespread opinion among successful minorities that they have had to put in extra hours and effort to achieve the same status as their white peers. This pervasive "we have to be better" mentality is hardly borne out of an empowering, inclusive culture.[98]

Stereotyping and devaluing are not relegated just to African-Americans. For some managers, there is the assumption that, if you are Latino, you are too social and, therefore, not as dedicated to your job. Sometimes the importance of family in Latino culture leads to the erroneous assumption that family comes before the job, which in turn interferes with attendance and produc-tivity. Women, too, are stereotyped and the object of unfair assumptions. The question of one's ability to travel comes up with women with children, single and married, far more often than it does with men in similar circumstances.

An unfavorable assumption or subtle bias can snowball over time without any act of conscious discrimination. Minority employees, for example, are often paid less than their counterparts. Assuming their qualifications, length of ser-vice and performance ratings are equal, how does this happen?

## A Hypothetical Scenario

It begins at performance review time several years earlier when a manager rates an employee (for purposes of this scenario, an African-American employee) lower than any of his non-African-American co-workers. The manager bases this rating and increase on some underlying assumptions that had little to do with productivity. Maybe he didn't like the fact that the employee wouldn't maintain eye contact or didn't participate in after-work activities, etc., etc. At any rate, the reason is not documented, and the employee's increase is 5% less than co-workers'. The next year, the same thing happens, even though there is a different manager. The reasoning goes something like this: "Well, if Bill gave Rodney less money, there must be a good reason. I'll do the same." And so it goes, year after year. By the time five managers have reviewed him, the employee is making 25% less overall than his peers, all done in little pieces along the way. Remember, this began with no valid reason, just an initial assumption. The disempowering effect of this all too common scenario is that a manager looks at low pay and "assumes" there must be something wrong with the employee, never questioning the system.

As does everybody, non-traditional managers also have limitations that must be considered in compensation, hiring, promotion decisions and disciplinary action. Ignoring a shortcoming and not creating a developmental plan devalues that employee and demonstrates a lack of integrity on the manager's part. Nevertheless, the limitations of non-traditional managers may still be a greater liability than the limitations of a traditional male manager.

## ENABLERS OF PRODUCTIVITY

Optimum productivity in an organization depends in large part on the quality of the work environment. Assuming that the foundation for diversity has been laid in an organization, there are a number of strategies companies can implement to impact productivity favorably. Three that are significant include the prevalence of teaming in the global economy, the growing support in companies for employee resource groups and the development of work/life programs.

## Teams

All kinds of teams are prevalent in today's workplace:

- Functional teams
- Cross-functional teams
- Multifunctional teams
- Global teams
- Co-located teams
- Virtual teams
- Self-managed teams

Even a team of two of the same ethnicity will have some diversity, because no two people process information or perform tasks in exactly the same way. The correlation between the diversity of a team and its ability to be creative and make sound decisions is higher than with a homogeneous team. The payoff for promoting diversity in teams is high. The sense of being a part of a cohesive and highly functioning team motivates people to be at work, thereby lowering absenteeism, achieving greater results and increasing productivity.

Flexibility that managing a diverse workforce requires also enhances an organization's ability to be nimble and implement change quickly, essential to remaining competitive. Time to execute in order to meet customer needs is generally reduced when the workforce is trained to understand and develop relationships with people of differing cultures.

Increasingly, organizations are relying on teams to create solutions. Although diversity on teams can sometimes slow decisions as they work through differences in perspective and experience, those decisions and solutions are usually better, more innovative and longer lasting.

Because customers like to deal with "someone like them" or at the very least someone knowledgeable about their needs and tastes (cultural competence), a trained diverse team ensures that the organization has its pulse on the market. Conversely, an organization that is dominated by one group can easily get out of touch with customers' requirements.

With a greater reliance by organizations on global teams to get work done, effective team dynamics is crucial. Negative behaviors reduce productivity.[99] Given the important role teams play as a primary interface with the diverse customer base, organizations committed to inclusion need to provide training to optimize the effectiveness and creativity of teams and counter negative team dynamics.

When a company fosters an inclusive culture based on trust, respect and opportunity and teaches people how to interact effectively with one another, they are likewise more adept at dealing with diverse customers. Team members are forced to "push the envelope" and challenge their comfort zones in forming relationships across differences. Sharing ideas, perceptions and experiences reduce assumptions and stereotyping about one's race, ethnicity or culture.

How can team success be optimized? O'Hara-Devereaux and Johansen offer rules of thumb to enhance global teams' success. They include:

- Create a common language and pace your communication. When the routine fails, information cannot flow. Details get lost.

- Use knowledgeable cultural consultants liberally. Realizing that you need help is a strength; knowing when to pull in experts is crucial.

- Build trust. Take time for relationships. Create the human "glue" necessary to support a team's success.

- Redesign work processes to suit the global environment. Surface different interpretations and perceptions. Find a "third way" to work.

- Manage with milestones. Without a mutually agreed to accountability, the team will fail.

- Be creative with technology. Technological infrastructure varies considerably in sophistication across the span of a global team.

- Be fluent with cross-cultural management practices. Flexibility in responding to a variety of cultural demands is crucial.

- Create "third way" strategies. The old way of doing things is culture-bound. New mindsets that reject "our way/your way" orientation need to reign.[100]

## Employee Resource Groups

These groups, which are comprised mostly of like individuals, go by different names:[101] affinity, networking, resource or advocacy groups; diversity or business teams, to name a few. Company support has grown for such groups over the years. It is common that most Fortune 100 companies and many others now market their endorsement of these groups in employment literature and on websites. It wasn't always so.

A few years ago there was still significant resistance by companies to these teams, which usually centered on fear that they would develop into complaint sessions with self-serving agendas, posing a potential liability for unfair labor practices. Another commonly raised concern, not entirely unwarranted, was one of "if we recognize one group, requests from others will mushroom. Where will we draw the line?" And, of course, there was always a question of how to manage these groups. More progressive companies, sensing that squelching such activity would only drive the group(s) underground and risk wider-spread dissatisfaction, agreed to work with teams in setting up guidelines.

## Guidelines

Guidelines usually have several common themes:

- The team's charter, goals and strategies must align with those of the business.

- A business plan is required to be submitted and reviewed for formal recognition.

- A high-level company officer should serve as the team's sponsor. (This person is often a white male, which is helpful to the team in gaining entreé and credibility with upper management and beneficial for him in learning about a culture and its issues.)

- The group does not serve as an advocate for an individual, but rather for the group as a whole, focusing on systemic issues that the group deems most important.

- Each group is open to all employees. This not only minimizes criticism of being closed or self-serving, it helps educate others and promotes trust, understanding and cultural competence.

- Membership is voluntary, since not all people of difference are interested in affiliating with such a group.

The benefits of supporting these groups are numerous both to the company and to the team members as well as to communities at large. They promote inclusion and retention. Groups provide a buffer between management and employees on sensitive issues and an infrastructure to address these issues in a proactive manner. Responsibility for meeting the needs of nontraditional employees is shared by management and groups.

One company that has demonstrated "staying power" with its diversity initiative is *Texas Instruments*. Since 1990, TI has recognized employee resource groups and supported them with funding and resources - an executive sponsor and a human resources partner. Their funding covers developmental needs (e.g., workshops, mentoring and networking) as well as speakers. TI regularly solicits input from these teams to provide solutions to business issues. Teams are also given funding for community outreach projects, which they are empowered to select and manage.

## Developmental Opportunities

Especially when there are no other mentoring or networking opportunities for people with difference, employee resource groups provide support and coaching, which, in turn, can positively impact retention. This may take the form of a monthly lunch, when a group of African-Americans, for example, can sit together without causing unwarranted speculation by observers. For some African-Americans, who may comprise a small percentage of the overall workforce and be scattered throughout departments, this may be the one opportunity to network with "someone like them."

Groups provide a "safe harbor" to openly discuss concerns and issues, often learning positive coping strategies from others who "have been there." Or, they can also use the group as a "reality check" to receive honest feedback from colleagues they trust, sometimes discovering that their issue is one of their own making that they need to address if they expect to progress in the company.

For leaders of the group there is opportunity to gain visibility with high-ranking management, practicing leadership and communication skills, serving as advocates, champions and spokespersons. Stalled careers can become "unstalled." Mentoring opportunities can arise. Future nontraditional leaders can be developed as they gain visibility to the expertise and decision-making skills of senior management as well as insight to corporate policies and "unwritten" rules that might otherwise have never surfaced for them.

## Advocacy / Advisory Opportunities

Employee resource groups can raise awareness of senior management of archaic policies or subjective, potentially unfair practices. Commonly, they work to improve major people systems like performance feedback, employee development interventions and bias-free recruiting. There is usually a very positive spillover when people systems are examined and improved. What's good for one group is usually good for all. Company leaders often use employee resource groups as sounding boards before major decisions are announced or to polish business strategy prior to release. This relationship can save the company money and embarrassment, especially where recruiting or ethnic marketing is concerned.

Group leaders often gain exposure and credibility as they assume the role of champion and spokesperson internally and externally on the subject of diversity. Business objectives are supported through participation in job fairs and community events. Leaders often act as spokespersons and liaisons with the community. Employee resource groups often sponsor in-house education and development programs. This promotes a company's ability to recruit diverse talent in a tough, competitive market. Supporting employee resource groups may be the most important factor in a company's ability to demonstrate commitment to diversity. In fact, one of the most important criteria potential recruits use in selecting a company is whether or not they support employee resource groups.

A warning: Company leadership must ensure that its support is real and not regarded as merely tolerance or paying "lip service" to diversity. They must be actively engaged, endorse and be accountable for cultural change and results. Otherwise, leaders risk diversity efforts being perceived as another "programme du jour." They also risk further frustrating, alienating, and retaining employees of difference as well as traditional employees who support diversity.

## Work/Life Programs

Productivity is also increased through implementation of work/life programs. Today's workplace demands that we blur the lines between work and play, sometimes creating a sense of isolation from family and a need for balance and resilience to be restored.

Work/Life balance is seen as a predominantly women's issue. Yet, the Families and Work Institute's recent National Study of the Changing Workforce found virtually no difference between women and men in levels of stress regarding parental versus professional commitments.[102] A recent study by the Radcliffe Public Policy Center found that for young men, work/life balance was more important than money, power or prestige.[103] A work/life survey conducted by *IBM* several years ago indicated that more men than women have difficulty balancing their work and personal lives. In both the U.S. and Europe, the IBM survey indicated that a key retention topic revolved around work/life issues.

In 1997, the Work & Family Connection organization, the Whirlpool Foundation and *Working Mother* magazine collaborated to conduct research about the effectiveness of work/life programs at over 150 companies to determine their impact on employee loyalty and productivity.[104] Not surprisingly, almost every effort to help employees with childcare issues has been successful in increasing morale, the most positive being emergency care for sick children in the employee's home. Survey respondents indicated that childcare assistance in the form of vouchers or on- or near-site services most impacted productivity. Lactation rooms encouraged mothers to return to work. Parenting and adoption seminars were successful in increasing morale. Providing eldercare referral information and/or case management reduced absenteeism.[105]

Regarding work/life programs, the survey found that flex scheduling, job sharing, compressed workweek and part-time work had the greatest response relative to positive impact on productivity. Of all options, telecommuting received the most enthusiastic endorsement.

Alternative work scheduling makes good business sense. It increases morale because it indicates to employees that the company is sensitive to their attempts to balance work/life issues. It helps businesses too. With flex scheduling, the company's daily coverage is extended, especially important in today's global economy when more and more business is done with people and companies in different time zones. It gives a company an edge when trying to recruit and retain talent. With telecommuting, in particular, overhead costs are reduced in savings on space, capital equipment and utilities. With decreased commuting, pollution is reduced.

Research indicates that work/life balance initiatives reduce stress-related illness in employees, which means less absenteeism and lower insurance premiums. *Johnson & Johnson*, for example, found that workers using flex time and family-leave policies were absent 50% less often than the workforce as a whole. For the company, ROI and productivity improve. People tend to "lighten up," and more humor amongst the workforce seems to be evident. Research also indicates that the company benefits even more than employees from flexible arrangements through reductions in tardiness and absenteeism, improvement in morale and retention and increased recruiting advantages.

## CHALLENGES AND OPPORTUNITIES

One opportunity that can be derived out of a diversity initiative is the growth and development of existing and future leaders. Strong leadership is key to optimizing productivity. The challenge is that traditional managers, largely white males, often feel left out of a diversity initiative. They don't buy in. They sometimes feel threatened. They are passively resistant. They need to be appealed to from a "what's in it for me" approach. In addition to diversity positively impacting the bottom line of their organization and enhancing their own personal recognition and reward, managers can become better leaders as a result of diversity.

Traditional managers learn from nontraditional managers and vice versa. With increased competition for leadership jobs that an inclusive culture fosters, white males are encouraged to perform even better, acquiring new skills and competencies. Much like the rest of the workforce, diversity helps them learn new approaches to problem-solving, new perspectives on issues, an openness they might not otherwise have acquired. The benefits for nontraditional managers are they learn business systems and gain insight to strategies and tactics that can enhance their personal success.

A learning environment creates recognition of micro-inequities and a resolve to challenge stereotyping and assumptions. A new sense of fairness is cultivated, particularly in assessing the continued appropriateness of policies and procedures or the introduction of new programs. Where many managers previously felt unprepared to manage diversity effectively, new competencies are acquired to ensure full participation and optimal development of all employees.

Emphasizing common ground and equal opportunity for all, diversity based on inclusion leverages the talent and experience of everyone, white male employees included. Empowerment grants every employee the capacity to be creative, productive and fully utilized. In this sense, diversity breeds cost-effective solutions. Addressing the issue of improving retention of women, for example, addresses that problem for everyone. Seemingly small "wins" actually whittle away barriers to empowerment and diversity without triggering non-productive backlash and resistance.

## CONCLUSION

A sound business practice is regular use of employee surveys to keep a pulse on issues that point to employee dissatisfaction and languishing commitment, usually precursors to decreased productivity and increased attrition. A strategy to assess the image and reputation of your company relative to its diversity practices amongst its most valued communities and stakeholders externally – potential recruits, customers and suppliers – is also strongly recommended.

There is a risk and cost factor associated with not paying attention. The ramifications of this risk are so huge and potentially damaging to a company that the proactive, positive steps outlined above that favorably impact productivity and profitability, become overshadowed.

I'm speaking of the giant polluted cloud that surrounds a company when it has not paid attention to the signs in the workplace of disempowerment, employee discontent and the negative impacts of exclusion-based policies. I'm speaking of the monetary and human costs to a company suddenly thrown into upheaval with negative long-term publicity, defensive posturing and the constancy of lengthy scrutiny, with all eyes watching and every move magnified. This occurs when a company's world is transformed into a glass house that is being shattered by a lawsuit.

## SUMMARY HIGHLIGHTS
# Business Imperative 7: Improved Productivity

- In an inclusive environment, the top priority is to optimize the potential of every employee through continuous skill acquisition and increasing levels of responsibility. When morale is high and people feel valued and successful, productivity improves.

- There are numerous factors that prevent productivity from being optimized in an organization. The most significant are conflict, underutilization of employees and disempowerment.

- Diversity and empowerment go hand-in-hand in enabling creativity and productivity. Organizational dysfunction occurs when either or both is missing.

- Factors in a workplace that disempower people include those everyday acts of exclusion, devaluation and discouragement that push people of difference down – or out.

- While blatant, intentional discrimination has mostly been eliminated from the workplace landscape, forms of highly subtle discrimination remain.

- People continue to be disempowered by managers' greater comfort in dealing with "people like them."

- Forty-five percent of minority executives stated they had been the target of a racial or cultural joke at work. Sixty-five percent of women of color in management left their jobs due to employers failing to address subtle gender and racial bias.

- Minority managers believe they spend more time in the "bullpen" waiting for their chance. Once they get that first "plum" assignment, often they have to prove themselves yet again.

- Ignoring a shortcoming and not creating a developmental plan devalues that employee and demonstrates a lack of integrity on the manager's part.

- When a company fosters an inclusive culture and teaches people how to interact effectively with one another, they are more adept at dealing with diverse customers.

- Supporting employee resource groups may be the most important factor in a company's ability to demonstrate commitment to diversity.

- The workplace demands that we blur the lines between work and play, sometimes creating a sense of isolation from family and a need for balance and resilience to be restored.

- Almost every effort to help employees with childcare issues has been successful in increasing morale, the most positive being emergency care for sick children in the employee's home.

- Flex scheduling, job sharing, compressed workweek and part-time work had the greatest perceived positive impact on productivity.

- The company benefits even more than employees from flexible arrangements through reductions in tardiness and absenteeism, improvement in morale and retention and increased recruiting advantages.

# BUSINESS IMPERATIVE #8:

## THE COST OF NOT PAYING ATTENTION

They ignored me, ignored me, ignored me to the point where I felt I had no other recourse.

- Greg Clark
  One of Original Plaintiffs
  1999 Coca-Cola Lawsuit[106]

## COSTS Of LITIGATION

Avoiding litigation has been one of the strongest inducements for implementing diversity. Even though diversity has a much more expansive definition than affirmative action or equal employment opportunity, awareness of the costs and risks to profitability that litigation poses, remains high on the radar screen of company management. The closure to a class-action suit, typically with findings for the plaintiffs and substantial remedies, does not end the damage to a company's reputation that can taint it for years.

## EQUAL EMPLOYMENT OPPORTUNITY

Equal Employment Opportunity is defined as the right of all persons to work and advance on the basis of merit, ability and potential. It is comprised of a group of fair employment laws that protect individuals from discrimination based on their race, color, religion, age, sex, sexual orientation, pregnancy, national origin, veteran status or disability.

Employment actions encompassed by these laws include hiring, training, promotion, discipline, transfer, layoff, termination and "all other terms and conditions of employment."

If plaintiffs feel they have been discriminated against in one of these employment activities and are a member of a "protected class," they have recourse to file a charge of discrimination with the Equal Employment Opportunity Commission (EEOC) or a local human rights agency with similar enforcement powers.

## AFFIRMATIVE ACTION

Government mandated, affirmative action requires companies with at least 50 employees and $50,000 in government contracts to take proactive measures to ensure equitable representation of women and people of color at all levels of the organization. It was adopted to promote the goal of Equal Employment Opportunity (EEO) and is grounded in moral and social responsibility to amend wrongs done in the past to people of color and women.

An annual written Affirmative Action Plan (AAP) is required and includes analysis of workforce representation and identification of problems in meeting suggested goals (not quotas, as is commonly misrepresented) and timetables. AAPs are also written to cover people with disabilities and Vietnam-era veterans.

The intent of affirmative action is to redress past and present factors that tended to systematically put some individuals in disadvantaged positions. The expectation is that companies will go beyond mere compliance and demonstrate "good faith efforts" to achieve equitable representation.

The Office of Federal Contract & Compliance Programs (OFCCP) enforces compliance with affirmative action requirements. Penalties can be severe and constraining to companies not found to be in compliance, ranging from monitoring a company's employment or compensation practices for some period of time to disbarment from any future government contract.

Affirmative Action addresses discrimination practices that inhibit equitable representation of protected classes. It was never intended to address equal access issues, workforce attitudes, employee development or corporate culture. Diversity does.

## DIVERSITY

Diversity initiatives are not government mandated. They are designed and implemented voluntarily by companies. Initiatives and the span of their framework and strategies vary according to the objectives and culture of the company. Some closely mirror the intent of affirmative action, focusing programs largely on women and people of color. Other companies expand their definition of diversity and consciously craft their initiative to be inclusive of the widest possible spectrum of differences. A broader definition helps people, including white males, see themselves included in the initiative. It offers employees a chance to connect, develop and fortify relationships.

Some believe diversity initiatives blur or minimize the still-existing issues of women and people of color. Past diversity chairperson for the Society for Human Resource Management, Lisa Willis Johnson, for example, believes "race was the sacrificial lamb to launch diversity and make it palatable to corporate America."[107] Those that have been historically excluded from career opportunities and progression may reject a diversity initiative as overly broad and, therefore, meaningless.

Representation goals, accountability and metrics are wholly the province of the company. Obviously, most companies understand that it's difficult to promote diversity in an environment where there isn't any. Thus, a common goal for most companies focuses on representation, which equates primarily to people of color and women. Others focus on creating a culture that fosters valuing employees, supporting authenticity and embracing differences to thrive and be successful.

The overriding objective of diversity initiatives is not solely about satisfying legal requirements. The focus turns inward to address the quality of the environment. Most diversity efforts involve a commitment to some level of cultural change that stresses valuing differences and managing them effectively that will result in garnering favorable public support and a reputation as an employer of choice. More enterprising companies are addressing diversity issues globally as well.

## Differences Between Managing Diversity and Traditional Practices of Equal Opportunity/Affirmative Action

|  | EEO/AA | Diversity |
|---|---|---|
| Emphasizes post-selection treatment issues such as development and ability to realize one's full potential | no | yes |
| Recognizes and emphasizes the impact of culture differences among groups on employee experiences | no | yes |
| Recognizes the need for organization change and change among members of the dominant culture group | no | yes |
| Emphasizes business economic reasons for having and managing diversity | no | yes |

| | | |
|---|---|---|
| Approaches diversity as an opportunity more than a problem to be solved | no | yes |
| Acknowledges a broad range of group identities and affects on employment | no | yes |

Source: Managing Diversity & Glass Ceiling Initiatives as Economic Imperatives

For some companies, diversity has been a welcome alternative to affirmative action, given the polarization that the latter has surfaced on occasion. Yet, diversity, too, has had its naysayers with many diversity professionals wanting to distance themselves from the diversity movement, calling themselves "inclusion specialists."

What we call the initiative and its champions is not as important as the benefits they bring: optimizing the potential of organizations and its employees.

## RISK FACTORS

In a culture that doesn't practice inclusion, there is more conflict and stress. Other manifestations of a culture that is ambivalent or chooses to ignore the benefits of diversity include:

- Higher Absenteeism

- More Health-related Illnesses

- Increased Leaves of Absence

- Languished Creativity and Productivity

- Deterioration in Customer Service

- Lost Customer Loyalty

- Increased Risk of Charges of Discrimination/Government Compliance Sanctions

- Tarnished Community Image and National Reputation

- Less Positive Perception of Shareholders and Investors

- Increased Risk of Litigation

## LAWSUITS

Lawsuits alleging employment discrimination increased over 300%, from slightly under 7,000 in 1990 to over 21,500 in 1998. Race, gender, age-based and harassment lawsuits are most frequent and most costly. As reliance on multinational teams increases and levels of management are reduced, the potential for conflict and harassment amongst coworkers loom. Likewise, the growing number of companies that are foreign-owned, operating in the U.S. and unfamiliar with American employment law, may contribute to increased litigation.

Complaints filed with the EEOC against employers increased in 2001 to almost 81,000, with age and disability discrimination allegations on the rise, not a surprise given an increasingly gray workforce. Race and gender complaints still account for the majority of allegations. According to the EEOC, more companies elected to settle cases in 2001 than in the past, to the tune of over $250 million.

According to a 2002 article in *Business Week*, judgments in discrimination suits are increasing.[108] The median jury award in employment practice cases rose 44% between 1999 and 2000, to $218,000. 20% of all verdicts topped $1 million, which doesn't include the cost of legal representation. It is estimated that 70% of plaintiffs win their cases once they get to court. Judges and juries tend to have less sympathy for the large corporation with deep pockets. High legal fees and settlements are characterized by the failing of companies to address diversity issues.

Most Fortune 500 companies have received complaints of sexual harassment. More than one-third have been sued. Litigation costs are only the tip of the iceberg. They do not include the costs of lowered morale, stress, absenteeism and attrition that increase when companies fail to address disempowering environmental issues.

Sybil Evans, a conflict management consultant, notes that most judgments run in excess of $1 million, which does not include the 10 to 15% additional costs in legal fees. She adds, "this is not to mention wasted management time, morale and lost productivity." [109]

Then there are the potential boycotts by consumers. In 1996 alone, *Avis, Mitsubishi, R.R. Donnelly* and the *United Dairy Farmers* were targets of boycotts by consumers because of alleged discrimination.

Early discrimination suits in the 1970s and 1980s largely revolved around hiring issues with regard to women and people of color. More recently, suits are likelier to involve issues of promotion and compensation for those employees at the same level as white males, as was the case at Texaco (see below). Large numbers of sexual harassment cases are still being litigated.

Few of the top companies in America have escaped the costs and embarrassment associated with discrimination lawsuits. Following is a random sample of some of the cases that endured the most notoriety and publicity. Each highlights a different, yet frequent, issue of litigation:

## American Express

In February 2002 a federal judge approved a $31 million settlement by American Express on an age and sex discrimination lawsuit. The suit was initially filed by four women in 1999, who were later joined by 13 more, in what became a class action suit covering 4,000 female financial advisors. The suit alleged that the women were unfairly denied promotions and pay increases. They further alleged that American Express created a "glass ceiling" for female financial advisers by giving lucrative accounts and leads on prospective clients to male advisers.

According to the lawsuit, it was also alleged that men were recipients of training, mentoring and promotions that were denied to women. American Express agreed to begin mandatory diversity training and hire a diversity officer for its financial advisers subsidiary. The company will also be monitored by the Equal Employment Opportunity Commission to ensure that a female representation goal of 32% is achieved. The incumbent female population is 25% at the time of this writing.

## Mitsubishi

In 1998, Mitsubishi agreed to settle a class action suit brought against them by the EEOC on behalf of 350 women at Mitsubishi's Normal, Illinois plant, which alleged a pattern of sexual harassment. Mitsubishi agreed to pay the plaintiffs $34 million.

Following the settlement, Mitsubishi officials pledged to "create a model workplace" and resolve any future sexual harassment claims quickly. Instead, the company allegedly intimidated the plaintiffs and failed to live up to the settlement, which called for an immediate return to work. As it turned out, only those on disability leave were given an opportunity to return to work. They reported delays in the processing of their paychecks.

Also ordered by the settlement was mandatory anti-sexual harassment training. It was alleged that during the training, jokes and inappropriate, harassing comments occurred with no consequences. The next year a three-foot cardboard penis was reportedly displayed in plain view of the plant.

As a result, activists with the National Organization of Women named Mitsubishi a "Merchant of Shame" and began demonstrations nationwide, distributing fliers throughout the U.S. reporting on the company's behavior.

The lesson learned here is that any global company doing business in another country must understand and comply with the employment laws of that country.

## Texaco

Probably no other litigation draws the correlation between the lack of paying attention to diversity and financial impact than Texaco. This case, more than any other, got the attention of CEOs, not so much because of the allegations, but because of the financial toll the case took against Texaco's bottom line. In 1994, a group of senior executives at Texaco were in a meeting, the subject of which was a class-action discrimination suit brought by nearly 1,400 African-American employees and managers who claimed they were denied promotions because of their race. Unfortunately for Texaco, the meeting was secretly taped by one of the participants, who, after being laid off, promptly handed over the tape to the attorneys representing the employees. On the tape, executives were heard to use racial slurs, including the "n" word, and casting aspersions on Kwanzaa, an African-American holiday. They were also heard plotting the destruction of documents demanded as a result of the lawsuit.

Two days after the allegations, Texaco's market capitalization dropped by about half a billion dollars.

The ensuing publicity was a public relations nightmare. Reverend Jesse Jackson referred to Texaco as the "Mark Fuhrman of Corporate America." The National Urban League and the NAACP called for boycotts of Texaco stations. Many stockholders chose to react by selling their stock, and the stock price dropped dramatically. Federal prosecutors launched a criminal investigation into obstruction of justice charges. The firestorm of publicity was so intense Texaco decided to settle the case out of court two weeks later for $175 million.

## Coca-Cola

Until recently, Coca-Cola had the reputation of being "diversity-friendly." In 1999, a class-action suit was filed against Coca-Cola on behalf of eight African-American employees who charged the company with discrimination in promotions, evaluations, terminations and pay. It was led by Cyrus Mehri, the attorney who won the settlement in the landmark Texaco case.

Six months after the initial lawsuit was filed, Coca-Cola's then CEO, Doug Ivester, demoted the company's top African-American executive, Carl Ware, who then announced he would retire. Ware was a key figure in Atlanta's African-American community. Four years earlier he had written a memo on how the company could help African-American employees rise through the ranks, most of which had not been acted upon by the time of the initial lawsuit.

When Ivester lost his job to successor, Doug Daft, Ware was unretired and promoted to executive VP for global affairs. Several of his recommendations were then implemented, including tying executive bonuses to effective management of diversity.

Coco-Cola settled the suit in November 2000, for $192 million and to its credit has quickly embarked on improving its record. Thus far, Coca-Cola has spent $500 million with diversity suppliers, implemented a formal mentoring program and created a series of diversity celebration days modeled on their ad, "We'd like to teach the world to sing."

Johnnie Cochran has since filed a new lawsuit against Coca-Cola on behalf of four new plaintiffs, asking $1.5 billion in damages.

The unfortunate lesson learned here is that perhaps all of this could have been avoided. Greg Clark, one of the original plaintiffs, has stated that he never would have sued in the first place if he'd felt his internal complaints were taken seriously and acted upon.

## LOSS OF REPUTATION

The costs associated with lawsuits come right out of the profit line. The ensuing loss of reputation that companies experience has additional costs, often long-term. A tarnished image negatively affects shareholder confidence. The stock price often declines. It increases unwanted curiosity on the part of government agencies with their own enforcement powers. It impacts existing consumer loyalty and spending, some of whom will bolt for products and services of competitors with stronger diversity commitments and a solid reputation.

Under the cloud of lawsuits, the ability to acquire new customers and suppliers can be limited. Employees are embarrassed, and their pride, loyalty and commitment (and thus, their productivity) are often lower. Potential recruits are less inclined to view the company as an employer of choice. The pervasive notoriety and recognition that companies dream of getting for free in good times are hardly desirable in bad.

However, recovery and turn-arounds are possible. *Shoney's* and *Denny's* are two such examples. Both were hit with substantial lawsuits involving race discrimination. Both suffered profuse negative publicity - even boycotts. With considerable effort and cost, both have managed to reverse the downward trend of public opinion. Advantica, parent company of Denny's, responded to its legal troubles with an aggressive effort in minority recruitment and diversity supplier procurement. For the past two years, it has been rated as the number one company on *Fortune's* list of Best Companies for Minorities to Work For! The individual with the largest number of Denny's franchises today is an African-American.[110]

As diversity consultant, R. Roosevelt Thomas, Jr. says on creating a diverse workplace: "the organization that has the greatest difficulty is the successful one." Few companies initiate such transformation on their own. According to Thomas, it takes great vision or great pain. For most, he says, "it takes pain."[111]

## CHALLENGES AND OPPORTUNITIES

How does a case like Texaco's happen 30 plus years after the Civil Rights Act was passed when 74% of all large companies in the U.S. are supposedly pursuing diversity initiatives? I believe it is because the commitment to diversity is weak and the changes largely cosmetic.

Much focus has been placed on diversity awareness training. In fact, many companies have been comfortable and lulled into thinking that training *is* the diversity initiative. Awareness alone does not cause change; and diversity training, while important, is merely a *component* of any initiative. To underscore the point, Texaco management had been through diversity training just prior to their lawsuit. Obviously, it didn't take.

While valuing diversity is good for people, it's the company that has the opportunity to reap the greatest rewards. But, if there is a lack of authenticity, commitment and staying power to the initiative on the part of its leaders, it can backfire, resulting in huge monetary and human losses and boundless missed opportunities in the marketplace.

Some companies, fearing a lawsuit, are immobilized by the perceived risk of implementing a diversity initiative. Some supervisors are unwilling to give accurate feedback on performance fearing that, if they say the wrong thing; they'll be sued.

There is a legal risk, to be sure, but it is not nearly so great as the costs associated with a manager ignoring his/her responsibility to ensure productivity and morale of the work group are optimized. Avoiding a difficult discussion is hardly modeling a behavior that reflects respect for the individual. An employee deserves to know when his/her performance is substandard. A culture that is committed to inclusion honors its responsibility to support that employee in restoring his/her performance to an acceptable level.

Creating a culture of inclusion enhances feelings of trust. Employees see changes in the organization and sense they are valued and respected for their competence and differing perspectives. Their willingness to take risk and assume greater responsibility increases, as does their loyalty to the organization. They have a vested interest in contributing to the success of the organization.

## CONCLUSION

An inclusive culture is characterized by an open environment, one that empowers employees to challenge the status quo and air grievances internally as opposed to going to a third party.

A focused, flexible organization committed to diversity principles remedies disempowering barriers to inclusion. When effectively managed, diversity can reduce the probability of discrimination-based litigation.

SUMMARY HIGHLIGHTS
# Business Imperative 8: The Cost of Not Paying Attention

- Avoiding litigation has been one of the strongest inducements for implementing diversity.

- In addition to litigation, there are numerous other risk factors that negatively impact the bottom line for companies that don't practice inclusion.

- Costs associated with lawsuits come right out of the profit line.

- The closure to a class-action suit, typically with substantial remedies for the plaintiffs, does not end the damage to a company's reputation that can taint it for years.

- A tarnished image negatively affects shareholder confidence. The stock price declines. Unwanted curiosity by government agencies is raised. Existing customer loyalty is tested and their purchasing suspended.

- Many companies have been lulled into thinking that training is the diversity initiative. Awareness alone does not cause change. Diversity training, while important, is merely one component of an initiative.

- When effectively managed, diversity can reduce the probability of discrimination-based litigation.

# BUSINESS IMPERATIVE #9:

# REINVENTING A REPUTATION FOR EXCELLENCE

Some people believe that seeking diversity automatically leads to excellence, but I think focusing on excellence inevitably leads to diversity.

> - William C. Steere, Past CEO
>   Pfizer[112]

## BECOMING THE BUSINESS OF CHOICE

What Rosabeth Moss Kanter discovered two decades ago still applies today. In her historic book, *The Change Masters*, she writes that a company with progressive human resources practices, such as diversity, has more long-term profitability and financial growth over a 20-year period than its counterparts.[113]

In addition to the potential of acquiring new business from the emerging markets of diverse customers, selling more product as a result, and generating business for diverse suppliers; engaging in these strategies enhances a company's reputation as a solid and respected corporate citizen. The payback is significant.

By creating trust in honoring its visible and on-going commitment to diversity, a company reaps the benefits of a continuously expanding customer and supplier base as well as a pipeline for future talent. The company not only becomes the "employer of choice," it becomes the "business of choice," joining that very select club of being one of the most admired companies doing business in the U.S. and globally.

## PROGRESS ON THE JOURNEY...

### Realizing the Vision

It's time to check back in with you. As you remember, your company was in serious trouble at the start of this journey. You've accomplished much since the start. Adopting a "pioneer spirit," you let your core values be what the authors of *Built to Last* call your "guiding beacon" on this visionary process.[114]

You began to understand the bottom-line advantages a diversity strategy would have on your business. Four years ago, you decided to implement a diversity initiative. You have taken to heart and implemented the business imperatives for diversity discussed in this book. You defined the direction of your company and planned the desired "future state" of your organization and its reinvented culture with diversity as its core. It began with a code of ethics, corporate mission statement and value proposition that all spoke to trust, respect, dignity, integrity and a commitment to inclusion. What specific changes have you stewarded?

Today, you've moved the initiative from vision to reality and transformed the organization into a high-valuing, high-functioning entity that is characterized by innovation, flawless execution and profitability. The going has not always been easy. The potential for derailment sometimes seemed imminent. But, as the primary sponsor and visionary for this initiative, you persevered. Dramatic, positive change and successful business results have occurred as a result. If you were to give the company a rating, it might still be shy of "outstanding," but you feel it deserves to be mentioned in the company of some of the finest, most respected corporations operating today.

After all, in the last several years since implementing the initiative, the company has received national recognition for its excellent retention effort and state-of-the-art work/life programs. It has been bestowed awards as one of *Fortune's* Best Companies to Work For (including for minorities) and one of *Working Mother's* Best Companies to Work For. Last year, it was awarded the prestigious Catalyst Award (considered the Baldrige Award for diversity). Earlier this year, the company was awarded the government's EVE Award for its demonstrated commitment to affirmative action. It was one of the first to receive AARP's award for hiring older workers.

Just last week, validating your belief that the company had earned the right to stand beside some of the best-in-class companies in the world, the editors of *Fortune* informed you that your organization has been selected as one of this year's ten most admired companies in the U.S. You have indeed been admitted to a very elite club, along with the likes of *GE, Cisco, Walmart, Southwest Airlines, Microsoft, Home Depot, Berkshire Hathaway, Schwab and Intel.*

## FORTUNE's 'MOST ADMIRED COMPANY' AWARD

The evaluation process for this award is unlike any other. You don't apply. There is no self-nomination option. Winning companies are selected by peers. Judges include 10,000 executives, directors and security analysts who are asked to rank companies who finished in the top 25% in the previous year as well as those that finished in the top 20% of their industry. While there is a process for rating a company, of paramount consideration to judges is the company's overall character and credibility - delivering what it promises to multiple audiences.

The criteria for selection in the top ten of the Most Admired Companies are rigorous. They are judged on eight, which include:

1. Innovation

2. Financial Soundness

3. Employee Talent

4. Use of Corporate Assets

5. Long-term Investment Value

6. Social Responsibility

7. Quality of Management

8. Quality of Products & Services

As you work with your public relations staff to prepare communication materials on receiving this prestigious recognition that will be distributed to employees, retirees, customers, shareholders, suppliers and business partners from around the world, you solicit feedback from *Fortune* as to why your company was selected.

Here are some of the comments from the judges for their rationale in selecting your company based on the eight key criteria:[115]

## 1. Innovation

"This company implemented a unique *'global intelligence initiative'* that created *competencies* necessary to conduct business successfully with the increasingly diverse cultures of the world and the multi-ethnic markets here in the U.S."

"This effort enabled the company to really get close to its customers, and, as a result, to *predict changes* in the marketplace and *adapt quickly* to these changes."

"The company has reinvented itself. Because its culture is viewed as empowering and inclusive, its retention rate is one of the highest in its industry. Its recruitment plan, which calls for far fewer hires due to *successful retention*, is forward-thinking and 'joined at the hip' with the business' five-year plan, which focuses on future *anticipated skill requirements.*"

"The most admired companies seem to perform at their best when the heat is on, consistently *delivering to shareholders, customers and employees.* This company leads the pack."

"Because of the stability in the workforce that a high retention rate fosters, leaders can focus their attention on running the business, not keeping their organization staffed up. This stability in turn causes a *continuity in product development, innovative design* with targeted, *continuous improvement* and *costs savings goals* being realized."

"This company has chosen to *reinvest* significant revenue in their R&D effort. Its exemplary rate of innovation has been maintained as measured by the company's annual number of *patents,* which continues to exceed any of its competitors."

"One of the reasons for this company's exceedingly good retention rate is the innovative *work/life programs* it has introduced over the past three years. The choices of *alternative work schedules* the company offers are considered the *benchmark.*"

"Their five-year technology map is updated every six months, *integrating customer requirements, long-term innovation goals and expectations for suppliers.*"

"The company made a handful of *savvy acquisitions,* put two lead scientists of diverse backgrounds on its executive committee and successfully leveraged *its respected brand name* into a faster-growing, more profitable organization."

"What product design award haven't they won?"

## 2. Financial Soundness

"In order to maintain the desired economic growth of the company, it did some scenario planning. The company designed a contingency plan to step up *productivity improvements* rather than relying on a pipeline of new workers that might not exist."

"The company has successfully coordinated ten joint ventures, mergers and *acquisitions* over the past five years with marginal resource or productivity losses compared to the norm. In all ten cases the transition and *merging of cultures* and the integration of people and systems has been quite smooth, contributing to profit margins that lead the industry. This can be attributed to good planning and good selection."

"Their *debt-to-equity ratio* is favorable as is their *net income as a percent of sales.* Correspondingly, this company's Standard & Poor credit rating is stronger than its competitors."

"Their net debt to capital is 30% vs. 65% for the industry. They have the *highest returns on capital* in the industry with an ROA of 20% vs. 7% for the industry. Their quality of earnings is excellent. Cash flow is twice net income."

"Unlike some of its competitors in the past few years, this company has not suffered the negative financial and publicity consequences of a *major lawsuit.*"

"Their *state-of-the-art information and communication network,* which fosters efficient and timely *information sharing,* has significantly *lowered operational expenses* while helping solidify the "team-based" corporate culture, domestically and globally."

## 3. Employee Talent

"Not only has this company designed a successful retention plan, it has also focused considerable effort on designing *development programs* for its workforce. A *learning environment,* based on trust and respect, is embraced, resulting in a uniquely well-rounded workforce. The company prides itself in *learning faster* than its competitors."

"Their development programs, all highly benchmarked, include *career development plans, mentoring, shadowing,* a *fast-track program for key talent,* a three-tiered *skills upgrade* training program, *advanced leadership training* (second only to GE's) as well as training programs in the following areas: *customer service, team effectiveness & conflict resolution, enhanced communication & presentations* and *six sigma*. In addition, they have developed a *cultural competency curriculum* that includes a focus on global cultural intelligence and domestic diversity cultural awareness, including behavioral interview training, accent reduction, selling to a diverse marketplace and sexual harassment. They insist that all training, not just diversity curricula, reflects an understanding and commitment to principles of inclusion."

"The company broke the code: they understood better than most the almost one-to-one relationship between training and *improved productivity*."

"They outlined expectations of leaders that included *'role-model' behaviors and skills*, which are covered in depth in the advanced leadership program. Leaders are rated on demonstrated use of these skills and behaviors. Their bonuses are tied to promoting diversity and cultural competence throughout their organizations."

"This company has developed the reputation of being the *'employer of choice.'* Its recruitment *costs per hire are lowest* in the industry. Why? Because employees don't leave a good thing. And their recruitment advertising costs are kept low as a result."

"The company creates priority around spending time developing and courting the *future employee pipeline* through various outreach programs. It also was one of the first companies to recognize the need to keep *aging workers* in the ranks to fill skill gaps, partnering with them to extend benefits and postpone retirement."

"It has designed a *succession plan* that ensures *equitable representation* of all its employees. The management team is comprised of *40% women* and *25% people of color*. Even its Board of Directors reflects more diversity than most companies, adding two women and two executives of color in the past three years."

*"Compensation and rewards are tied to individual AND organizational performance* and profitability. Last year, more employees were evaluated as *peak performers* and more merit bonuses were awarded than in any previous year in the history of the organization."

Promotions are tied to optimized performance. Employees ('associates') are encouraged to stretch their personal development goals to prepare for future, more responsible positions and avoid skill *obsolescence. Performance management* is a high priority."

"Based on an annual *employee survey* and quarterly *focus groups* that measure any barriers to empowerment and inclusion, like discontent, being devalued or underutilized; the workforce appears to have great *pride* in and *loyalty* toward their organization. Employees appear to love their work ('happy jobs') and *have fun.*"

"Because employees are made to feel *highly valued,* they are given meaningful and *challenging work.* Diverse employees flock to this company due to its long-standing commitment of using *employee resource groups* to help run the business and the exemplary representation of women and people of color throughout its ranks."

## 4.  Use of Corporate Assets

"The company anticipated sooner than most that the *labor shortage* would impact its ability to be fully staffed at all times. This resulted in a 'full-court press' to develop an outstanding *retention program,* which emanated out of its global diversity initiative that began four years ago."

"*Costs saved* through retention and a resulting need for *fewer new hires* and *less training* have contributed to reduced operating expenses and three years of increasing, unsurpassed profits. *Knowledge capital* has been preserved."

"Three years ago they announced a 25 million share repurchase, an advantageous use of capital. The *stock rose* 50% within six months of the share buyback."

"This company has led their industry by recognizing that capital is more than dollars and equipment. Capital also comprises *people and their skills.* The company has invested at twice the rate of competitors, realizing twice the productivity as a result."

## 5. Long-Term Investment Value

"It recognized sooner than most the **huge** opportunity that courting a *multicultural market* here and abroad would bring, resulting in a clear leadership position in the sector in what promises to be the major growth markets of the future."

"This company has developed and solidified customer relationships better than most. I believe this is due to their *global intelligence initiative*, which enables them to really understand the needs of their customers."

"They have more than *doubled market share* in the past five years, increasing it from 15% to 35%, half of which has come from multicultural markets, with the promise of continued growth over the next decade."

"They have written the book on how to keep customers and shareholders happy, and their incredibly *strong culture of customer service* has increased the *loyalty* of their customer base, which should continue over the next decade."

"This company substantially *outperformed* their sector in fostering a diverse environment conducive to innovation and out-of-the-box thinking. The pipeline of *new products* is strong. New products generated over one-third of annual sales last year alone."

"The company's *rate of return* on initial investment over a five-year period is 150%, the highest by far amongst its competitors. This can be attributed to their commitment to a flatter, decentralized, more *efficient organization*, an *empowered and diverse workforce* that is exceptionally well-trained and a cadre of leadership that is unsurpassed in the industry."

## 6. Social Responsibility

"This company is consistently viewed as one of the most *integrity-based* and *socially responsible* companies around. Their code of ethics is embraced globally."

"It learned early on the value of designing a *procurement effort* that included identifying and courting a *diverse supplier base.* They were recently admitted as a member of the Billion Dollar Club, exclusive to those companies that award the most business to diverse suppliers."

"This company has brilliantly used its commitment to and relationships with suppliers around the world as a valuable avenue to *develop new customers.* More importantly, it has shared the wealth and *created opportunity for small businesses* worldwide, which, in turn, expands their *purchasing power* to buy more product."

"There is no company that exemplifies *public sector commitment* better than this one. The company sponsored 250 *internships* for high school teachers last summer to expose them to the skill requirements of their industry and improve the teachers' literacy in technology. Teachers who participate in the program are expected to proactively advise students in career choices that *meet the skill needs of industry.*"

"In an effort to *lower drop-out rates* and help students excel in math and science, company employees act as 'evangelists' for learning, *tutoring* students at risk. In the last five years its foundation has increased grants three-fold to support acquisition of *math and science* skills. The company has awarded 600 four-year college *scholarships* to provide incentives to at-risk students to graduate from high school and college. Their only criterion is that the student *major in math, science or engineering.*"

## 7. Quality of Management

"The bench at this company is deep and diverse. They are held accountable for developing the *future leaders* of the company. *Career planning* and feedback sessions are held quarterly. The *succession plan* is reviewed annually with upper management, ensuring there is equitable representation amongst future leaders. *Bonuses* are tied to achieving diversity goals in the leadership ranks and displaying behaviors and skills that foster inclusion."

"Management has done an excellent job on *reinventing its culture.* A culture of opportunity and success has been created, grounded in practicing the *'platinum rule.'* As a result, the culture is more spirited, more creative and more humane because of its value for *diversity and inclusion.*"

"Of note is the organization's tenacious commitment to *communicating* frequently on financial performance and the state of the business. Their strategic planning process incorporates a *tops-down, bottoms-up* approach, resulting in a concise, integrated summary of the company's progress."

"Any *distinction based on status* (e.g., badges, titles, dress, office space, even compensation) has been all but *eliminated.*"

"This company encourages *healthy debate* and *risk-taking. Conflict is minimal,* and *interdependence* is the accepted norm."

"Creating flatter organizations has ensured that *access to decision-makers* is open and welcomed. In actuality, *decision-making* has largely been *decentralized,* much of it driven down to its *global customer teams.* Teams are empowered to make decisions about scheduling, assignments and conducting peer reviews."

"*Leadership competency* is a true differentiator for this company. Leaders demonstrate the ability to collaborate transnationally. They can effectively manage cross-functional teams and quickly identify and change existing paradigms that create barriers to efficient work-flow."

"In addition to demonstrating a high degree of *multicultural competence,* leaders tend to be more *flexible and empowering.* Rather than changing players, they are more likely to change the rules when the rules no longer work."

"Managers hold high expectations for their employees. Their behaviors and skill set motivate employees to *achieve to their potential,* while maintaining an orientation to *continuously improving business results.*"

## 8.  Quality of Products & Services

"*Customer satisfaction* surveys are at an all-time high. Largely comprised of self-managed global teams, the workforce is empowered to make decisions, expected to solve problems quickly and hold themselves accountable for results."

"This company became one of the elite in quality management when it won the *Baldrige Award* two years ago."

"The company's global customer teams have earned a reputation of being *creative and responsive to customer requirements*. They are seen as highly trained with a depth and range of skills the competition would love to recruit."

"Their supplier management program earned a 'best in class' rating in an independent evaluation of performance in 20 benchmarked areas, including *diversity supplier procurement*."

"The company has received numerous *awards from customers*, far outpacing the competition. Even the president gets involved, devoting over 30 weeks a year to visiting customers."

"The company has also been recognized for its work in minimizing the digital divide and *improving the quality of life for the disabled, the elderly* and *the illiterate*. For this effort, they were awarded the coveted Access Engineering Award and the daVinci Award."

"Recently, the company received the Apple Design Award for its work in *demystifying math* for middle-schoolers."

"Last year, the company's *recruitment website* was given the gold award from the World's Best Websites organization."

"They won the Design Week 2001 Award for *editorial design* of last year's annual report, which featured its successful diversity initiative."

## RETURN ON INVESTMENT

The positive response from employees, customers, shareholders and business alliance partners to the selection of being one of the most admired organizations operating in the world today will provide paybacks to your company for many years to come. Here's how:

1. You recognized the need to embrace diversity and *utilize* it to your advantage, not just to accommodate it.

   As CEO you realized that in a global economy, *diversity is a means of creating wealth*. You were the driver behind your leadership team setting three priority goals relative to diversity:

   • Courting the ethnic, multicultural markets here and abroad.

   • Creating diverse representation at all levels within the organization (e.g., *seeking out differences*, not merely tolerating them)

   • Fostering the growth of diversity suppliers globally. (This latter effort built trust in the diverse communities in which the company operates, which, in turn, led to increased sales and recruiting capability).

2. You set about reinventing the company's *culture* to one based on inclusion, empowerment and customer service. You directed the leadership team to flatten and decentralize the organization to create previously unrealized efficiencies. You asked them to focus on developing competent, responsible and innovative multinational teams.

   A key priority for you was to identify and institutionalize inspiring values - trust, unconditional acceptance and respect for *all* people. You believed that, only with these values, could the company achieve increased organizational commitment and unbridled innovation and excellence in everything the company attempted.

3. You implemented a *diversity initiative* that included a comprehensive training program. A commitment to *lifelong learning* was framed by a priority that all employees would acquire global intelligence and *cultural competence*. You set an expectation that leaders demonstrate cultural literacy and role-model behaviors that inspire excellence in

performance, synergy and execution. You called for a comprehensive curriculum that ensures that underutilization of employees and skill obsolescence are minimized. This organizational commitment to development continues to sustain productivity improvements and creativity.

4. You had a vision that the company would be an "*employer of choice,*" a place where employees of all diversity would flock and remain. You courted a future employee pipeline that included previously ***undertapped constituencies,*** such as aging and disabled workers, and continued its support of developing math and science skills in middle and high school students.

   You called for state-of-the-art work/life programs to support a successful retention initiative. This enabled staffing efforts to be focused on future needs, not replacements, at considerable cost savings.

   Much of the success of your company resides in the fact that it is ***nimble*** in ***predicting*** and ***adapting*** to changing requirements in the marketplace. This ability can be directly attributable to lessons learned in overcoming resistance to the diversity initiative, where fomenting and sustaining change was sometimes difficult. As a result, the company is better positioned to tackle resistance other kinds of change will present your organization in the future.

## CONCLUSION

Your company is one that has created an extraordinary advantage for itself: wealth for its global stakeholders – its employees, investors, suppliers, customers and business partners.

It enjoys a reputation of excellence for its products, its execution and its relationships in the workplace and externally with customers and global partners.

As a by-product of its commitment to diversity, your company has created something even greater for its stakeholders than what existed before – *a sense of community* and *interdependence.* You've led your company through this extraordinary journey of change and created wealth without compromising your core values or your belief in and respect for people.

SUMMARY HIGHLIGHTS
# Business Imperative 9: Reinventing a Reputation for Excellence

- By creating trust in honoring its visible and on-going commitment to diversity, a company reaps the benefits of a continuously expanding customer and supplier base as well as a pipeline for future talent.

- In order for diversity to contribute to profitability, it must be used as an **advantage**, not merely accommodated.

# BUSINESS IMPERATIVE #10:

# A CULTURE WITH SOUL

There were never in the world two opinions alike; anymore than two hairs or two grains. The most universal quality is diversity.

- Michel de Montaigne
  French Essayist[116]

## CREATING CULTURAL AUTHENTICITY

Before bringing closure to this phase of the journey, it is important to examine **core values** and **key learnings** that helped shape and sustain your diversity initiative to produce the success it has thus far. Only through understanding these dimensions of diversity and the behaviors they command can an initiative have authenticity and meaning.

## DEFINITION OF DIVERSITY

In order to capitalize on the benefits of a culture based on inclusion, it is important that an organization *frame diversity broadly*. If a culture is to motivate and facilitate creativity and productivity in the workplace, it must appeal to the widest possible constituency base. A broader definition of diversity attracts a wider array of stakeholders – existing and future employees, customers, suppliers, business partners and stockholders. People must see themselves in the definition. Otherwise, widespread skepticism, resistance and a sense that espoused corporate commitment about diversity is just another "programme du jour" prevails.

A definition of diversity must include core differences – those aspects of our -selves which are *visible* as well as those *less visible* differences. Together these dimensions of diversity speak to our uniqueness and constitute the necessary framework in which diversity needs to be defined.

### Visible Differences

The core differences are those characteristics that impact us significantly in early socialization. They are aspects of ourselves which we cannot alter. These primary dimensions cannot be denied, for they are there for all to see – such characteristics as gender, color, age and many physical disabilities. Yet, focusing solely on them can limit and even undermine a diversity initiative.

Federal laws impose necessary nondiscrimination and affirmative action obligations on employers. For an initiative to be successful, however, organizations need to go *beyond traditional boundaries* of defining diversity in a historical context of affirmative action and "protected classes," based on *visible differences*.

In order to claim status as an inclusive company, an organization needs to increase definition bandwidth to include *all dimensions of differentness*, keeping in mind that there are differences within each difference.

## Invisible Differences

The more *intangible differences*, factors such as religious beliefs, job function, education, work experience, geographic origin, diversity of thought, etc., are aspects of ourselves we have the power to choose or change. While less influential on individual development than core dimensions, these secondary elements nevertheless play an important role in shaping an individual's values and experiences. These characteristics need to be included in an organization's definition of diversity. In an open, inclusive culture, acknowledging invisible differences is as important as acknowledging the more visible ones. Unlike the more tangible differences, these are the characteristics that are common to *all* people, regardless of their core visible differences, creating an opportunity for shared experience and discovery. The clarity and understanding emanating from this discussion can produce comraderie, interdependence and a unity of purpose.

Together, core and secondary dimensions of our diversity define our uniqueness.

## BARRIERS TO INCLUSION

### Cultural Lenses

Cultural lenses are the filters that serve to keep us stuck in our worldview. Everyone views the world differently. No two people see things in exactly the same way. We are conditioned through our inherited values, acquired beliefs, unique experiences and life learning to frame and align our worldview accordingly. These cultural lenses affect our assumptions, behaviors, decisions and expectations. They are often *unconscious.* They are often based on *ethnocentrism,* a propensity to see the world through a narrow view and judge others by what is familiar. An ethnocentric individual believes that one's own group is superior to all others.

For example, a *meritocratic lens* is one often exemplified in the workplace, particularly by members of the dominant culture. This set of lens embraces the perspective that:

- You kill what you eat.

- You get what you want because of hard work and making sacrifices.

- Cream rises to the top.

- There are no barriers to success.

- You just have to be willing to work hard enough.

- I persevered and overcame barriers. So can you.

Little awareness of the privileges awarded to members of the dominant culture or of the real barriers to a person of difference is demonstrated when these lenses are worn.

Organizations that are inclusion-based build gatekeepers into their structure to keep the effects of cultural lenses in check in their cultures.

## Privilege

Members of the dominant culture may inherit privileges that are unearned and arbitrarily awarded by society and organizations. Most recipients of these privileges are *unaware* of their existence or choose to remain oblivious. Privilege reminds us that we do not live in a true meritocracy; rather, a hierarchy of privileges exists. Our accomplishments are sometimes due to unearned privileges, based on our gender, age or color, rather than individual ability.

For example, most whites in this country are not concerned about being the targets of racial profiling as they drive down the highway or through an affluent neighborhood. They aren't concerned because, generally speaking, they don't need to be. In the workplace, whites don't worry about putting their ethnicity on the line when they're given a visible, challenging assignment with a risk of failure. Nor are they frequently asked to speak for everyone in their ethnic group. Not so for minorities in this country, particularly African-Americans.

Privilege perpetuates dominance and gives unearned and unfair advantages to members of the dominant culture.

## Labeling

*Stereotyping* is a rigid judgment we form as children growing up. It is a fixed, distorted generalization made about all members of a particular group. In other words, stereotyping blocks our ability to perceive an individual accurately.

How does stereotyping occur? In an effort to manage data being received, we form categories. We *create labels* in order to simplify a complex mass of data. No matter what information is available to our senses, we have learned to screen much out. Categorizing becomes an unconditional response.

We must be cognizant of mistakenly labeling someone based on his/her behavior when that behavior is encouraged in the individual's culture. For example, it is not uncommon in some Asian cultures to be reserved and respectful. This behavior is often misinterpreted in western cultures as showing a lack of interest or appropriate assertiveness. Similarly, Latinos, who are known to be very dedicated to their families, are often mislabeled as not giving work the priority it deserves. As Ann Morrison notes, "stereotypes make it acceptable among some traditional managers to ignore, disparage or discount the qualities and contributions of non-traditional managers."[117] Careers can be derailed when stereotypes are allowed to operate.

## Pre-judging

With stereotyping, prejudice often follows. *Prejudice* is the human tendency to see differences as weaknesses or deficiencies. Prejudice prevents us from seeing others in a non-judgmental way. Worse, it enables us to turn differences into liabilities. While we may not speak openly about our prejudices (and we all have prejudices), we may subliminally support prejudices. For example, while we might not openly express our opinion that managers of color, for example, are less competent than traditional managers, we could still think it and act on that belief.

Research shows that even people who want to avoid bias are often *conditioned* to an unconscious biased response. Ann Morrison conducted an experiment with hiring managers, all Caucasian, who were given resumes and photos of job applicants and asked to define what jobs they might offer these candidates. The resumes were identical. The pictures were different: an African-American male, an African-American female, a Latino, a Latina, a Caucasian male. The hiring managers typically assigned administrative jobs to women and line jobs to the men. Just to measure how pervasive prejudice can be, new hiring managers, this time all women of color, were asked to perform the same task. They made the same job assignments.

When we pre-judge people who are different from ourselves, our level of comfort may be maintained, but the opportunity to discover commonalities and likenesses is minimized. Our chance to expand our worldview and cultural lenses and broaden overly narrow paradigms is lost.

We must be vigilant not to pre-judge individuals, often unconsciously, based on their group identity. Generalizations based on group characteristics ignore the uniqueness of the individual (e.g., the differences within a difference). Acquiring cultural competence keeps false assumptions based on differences and stereotypes in check.

## Collusion

In *conscious or unconscious collaboration with others* or *collusion,* stereotypes, attitudes or behaviors of a particular group are reinforced. Collusion occurs on a regular basis. It's common because we are conditioned as children to modify our behavior in order to "fit in" and meet the expectations of peers, teachers and parents. We are socialized to give preference to our need to belong and to not feel like an outsider over other needs or opinions we may have.

We encounter *silent* forms of collusion in the workplace when we ignore an inappropriate joke or racial or gender-based slur. By not speaking up, we are reinforcing an exclusion-based culture and a disempowering status quo.

*Active, participatory* forms of collusion exist as well. Telling or laughing at that joke is one example. Hosting and/or participating in exclusion-based networking activities (e.g., golf, week-end outings, etc.) is another. Rumor-mongering is yet another (e.g., he only got that job because he filled a quota or she got that job because she ...).

# ELIMINATING BARRIERS TO INCLUSION

## Organizational Gatekeeping

A highly functioning organization recognizes when the disempowering effects of cultural lenses are in operation and provides education and tools to its leaders and employees to *monitor and counteract them.*

An organization that values peak performance creates an open, safe environment that encourages authenticity. Having the freedom to be yourself promotes credibility and trust in an organization. Trust and respect unleashes unconventional ideas and wisdom that positively impact competitive advantage and profitability.

Respecting differences and being inclusive translates to organizational norms of suspending judgment and seeking first to understand before making a decision.

## The Platinum Rule

A good rule of thumb in an inclusion-based culture is to view *everyone* as different. That way no assumptions can be made. We know that appearances can be deceptive. People who at first glance appear similar to us, are often quite different. And the opposite is equally true. By suspending judgment we create an opportunity for increased awareness and cultural competency. We learn more about ourselves and our culture in the process.

The golden rule, a revered practice and the foundation of many of our institutions, does not go far enough in today's multicultural world to acknowledge people's differences and uniqueness. The platinum rule helps us honor and value differences in others as well as in ourselves:

> *Treat others as they want to be treated.*

Being able to discuss and compare differences is the first step in valuing them, a far more enriching experience than labeling or judging.

## Cultural Competence

It is part of our human nature to gravitate toward and have more positive regard for someone who "looks like us." There is a greater level of comfort.

We assume that their sphere of experience and worldview is similar to ours. The only way to break out of this comfort zone is to seek out and learn from other people, from different cultures. This is a *conscious,* active exercise to expand *our cultural lenses*, worldview or understanding. This is how we acquire cultural competence.

## ESTABLISHING ACCOUNTABILITY

The implementation of metrics to evaluate the effectiveness of diversity initiatives will go a long way toward diluting resistance characterized by some business leaders today. Diversity initiatives have frequently been criticized for relying on subjective, qualitative data to support claims of success rather than developing quantifiable metrics that have more credibility with business leaders. There are several reasons for this.

Some diversity leaders have resisted using objective measures, believing that such metrics are inappropriate for such a "humanistic" initiative as diversity. Secondly, it has been challenging historically for diversity practitioners to identify and incorporate statistical methodologies in measuring the results of their work. Somehow, an unnecessary mystique about statistics has been created, and we've made it harder than it needs to be. The result has been a flight from quantifiable measurement.

Yet, lack of measurement tends to promulgate the perception that diversity is "soft," merely the "right thing to do," as opposed to a business initiative that can impact profitability and competitive advantage. A lack of metrics also contributes to a less than positive reputation of diversity practitioners that they neither understand numbers nor recognize what a critical success factor they are to any business initiative.

Diversity practitioners have a real opportunity to proactively change a current paradigm about diversity initiatives that holds that metrics are unimportant and/or elusive. Developing metrics will increase credibility, commitment and follow-through efforts in support of the initiative. Metrics will make communicating success and the value of the results in bottom-line terms much easier and much more compelling. (For an in-depth discussion of Metrics, see Appendix III).

## THE ROLE OF LEADERS

The roles that leaders play in an inclusive culture cannot be overstated. The vision and value proposition of a company establish the foundation and guiding principles by which the organization will govern itself. Leaders demonstrate and model the competencies and behaviors that support these principles. In the case of a company committed to inclusion, those values include trust, openness, dignity, respect, fairness, integrity and empowerment.

A company's commitment to diversity actually improves its *quality of leadership*. Inclusion, as we've learned, means seeking out differing perspectives and approaches to work and valuing the variety of insights a diverse workforce brings. It fosters discipline in remaining objective and open to all points of view and creating a culture that is supportive and interdependent. This goes beyond mere tolerance to a higher level of modeling unconditional respect and an overriding belief in the potential of people.

Leaders who appreciate differences fight dominance and presumed superiority in order to optimize opportunity and encourage full contribution of all employees. They set high standards for everyone, stimulating personal development and greater responsibility by creating learning opportunities that increase productivity, innovation and success, both for the individual as well as the company.

## FINAL THOUGHTS

You've created wealth for your organization and your stakeholders. You've developed a sense of community and interdependence in your company. What's left? Could you go further on this journey? If you took your organization to the next level, what would it look like? What possibilities could you create?

Vision your organization as the cosmopolitan company with **soul** –

- one that has embraced the *best* of *all cultures.*
- one that manages for profit as well as the *common good.*

... Continuously raising the bar.

... Positioned to prosper for years to come.

... Leaving an "indelible imprint" and creating a better place along the way.[118]

... Taking aim at the digital divide.

... Improving the economic standards and quality of life for people in the global communities in which you operate.

Yours can be a company that eliminates barriers that obstruct opportunity for human potential and human connectivity and creates *heightened affiliation and loyalty* amongst employees, stakeholders and customers – a condition much needed in today's workplace, and even more in tomorrow's.

... Becoming a "crown jewel" amongst visionary companies.[119]

... Putting people and product *before* profit.

... Freeing up the collective spirit of the inhabitants of our small planet, who, because of their differences, make this world *richer and wiser*.

You can cultivate a legacy in your company of having unconditional faith in *the power of differences* to create continuous and extraordinary business success in a *global culture* of *inclusion, respect* and true *meritocracy*.

Will your journey continue?

# SUMMARY HIGHLIGHTS
# Business Imperative 10: A Culture with Soul

- To capitalize on the benefits of an inclusive culture, an organization must frame diversity broadly.

- Many barriers to inclusion exist in the workplace. To be successful, companies must address and eliminate them.

- Organizations need to operate by the "platinum rule."

- Developing metrics will increase credibility, commitment and results. Metrics make communicating success much easier and much more compelling.

- Leaders must role model the competencies and behaviors that support diversity principles.

# APPENDIX I:

# SETTING UP A DIVERSITY INITIATIVE

Companies that recognize the strategic value of human capital are the companies that succeed. In today's marketplace, where a company's competitive edge is its people, top U.S. companies agree that a .... [diversity initiative] ... means a significant impact on the bottom line.

- Helen G. Drinan, Past President & CEO
  Society of Human
  Resource Management[120]

# SUCCESS FACTORS

If you've questioned whether diversity initiatives work, a recent survey of the Fortune 1000 list of companies conducted by the Society for Human Resource Management indicates that 91% of the respondents believed diversity initiatives help to maintain competitive advantage.[121] Additional benefits to a diversity initiative include:

| Factor | % Respondents |
|---|---|
| Improvement in Corporate Culture | 83 |
| Better Employee Morale | 79 |
| Higher Employee Retention | 76 |
| Better Recruitment | 75 |
| Decreased Complaints/Litigation | 68 |
| Encourages Creativity | 59 |
| Decreases Interpersonal Conflict | 58 |
| Facilitates New Markets | 57 |
| Improves Client Relations | 57 |

If an organization wants to make a commitment to creating a culture that utilizes its diversity as a competitive business advantage, there are factors that are necessary to ensure that the initiative is launched, managed and sustained effectively.

## New Perspectives

Before a diversity initiative is launched, some myths need to be acknowledged and replaced by different perspectives if the potential for success is to be optimized:

- The focus of a diversity initiative needs to be on changing the organization's culture, *not* the individuals in it.

- Diversity is *not* a problem to be solved. It is a process to be managed.

- Diversity begins with numbers, but it is *not just* about representation. ***Numbers alone do not cause change.*** And increased awareness (e.g., a diversity training program) alone does *not* create a level playing field. Diversity is not EEO or Affirmative Action.

- Focus and commitment needs to be *long-term.* There is a tendency for people to "want to arrive without the experience of getting there."

- Begin an initiative by embracing the diversity represented in the organization. Avoid a common tendency of wanting to *"go global,"* promoting international diversity without first doing the work to achieve an inclusive culture in the organization at home.

- The definition of diversity needs to be *broad* and inclusion-based (see Dimensions of Diversity model). Diversity is not just about race and gender, but it must include race and gender. The effort must welcome and include white males, whose needs must also be addressed. Without their support, the initiative will fail.

- Diversity is not owned by the HR department. Responsibility lies with leaders and employees, especially leaders.

## Enabling Strategies

- Sponsors of the initiative need to be guided by the principles of *long-term, planned* organizational change. Because change is so unsettling, a diversity initiative can feel like cultural derailment. It often feels worse before it gets better. Managing diversity is a *journey,* not a quick change to a policy or practice or merely offering a diversity awareness class.

- *Systems thinking* needs to be utilized in designing an initiative. Understanding the interconnectedness of the subsystems in an organization (e.g., how various parts of the whole interact and effect one another) is critical. The best strategies, implementation and communication plans will not always anticipate the dysfunctional outcomes that sometimes surface when an initiative is launched. It is unwise to deal with one sub-system in isolation, because other subsystems may respond in an unstable and unanticipated manner.

- Strong and *visible commitment* from leaders, especially at the top, is essential.[122] The success of a diversity initiative requires proximity to sources of power and establishing alliances that enhance power and increase results.

- To optimize buy-in and understanding and minimize the risk of the initiative feeling like a "programme du jour" or something "*being done to them,*" *employees need to be involved* and be able to influence the change process.

- Diversity must be understood as a *business issue,* one that aligns with business goals and objectives and results in increased organizational effectiveness. The need for a *business case* is imperative.

- The initiative must spell out how leaders will be held *accountable.* Their participation as *role models* for appropriate skills and behaviors is crucial. An *added incentive,* such as tying leadership bonuses to achieving stated objectives may need to be implemented.

- *Metrics* are needed to keep the initiative on track.

If your company is global, the initiative must also be framed with a *global perspective.* As in the U.S., diversity means different things to different people of the world. In the language of many countries, the word "diversity" does not exist. In others, diversity may not be recognized as a societal or workforce issue, much less as a strategic business initiative to increase organizational effectiveness and performance. Therefore, a global implementation plan needs to be *flexible,* taking into account *cultural norms and expectations* that are different in each country.

# RECOMMENDED FRAMEWORK

Twenty years ago Tom Peters and Robert Waterman in *In Search of Excellence* introduced the McKinsey 7S Model to identify the seven interdependent variables of an organization[123]. Edward Hubbard in his 1997 seminal work, *Measuring Diversity Results,* has expanded their model and added two additional variables. Dr. Hubbard designed the *Diversity 9-S Framework* model to assist organizations in examining their diversity change efforts to ensure they are in alignment with and are effectively supporting key organizational business goals. What follows are this author's recommendations of elements needed to frame a successful diversity initiative based on the 9S Model.[124]

## 1. Strategy

The initiative's overall diversity strategy is the link within the organization's units. It provides the *overall roadmap* and explains the diversity policy, the reason for the initiative, the process and the objectives. It is **THE PLAN** and includes tactics to enroll stakeholders, integrate and institutionalize the concepts, skills and results of the initiative into the organization as well as address resistance and sustain momentum.

The *roles* leaders and employees will play is described. How commitment and support will look in terms of competencies and behaviors expected in an inclusive culture are defined.

A decision as to whether the diversity initiative will be a new, stand-alone initiative needs to be made early on. If so, a comprehensive *implementation plan and timetable* are developed to support the strategy. In some cases, it might make better business sense for a company to forge an *alliance* with an *existing initiative,* such as TQM, which focuses on components such as customer satisfaction, teamwork, problem-solving and empowerment, that are similar to those included in a diversity initiative. The value of this approach is the alliance builds on current knowledge in the organization and helps ensure *systemic, cultural change.*

A key criterion for success is the development of a sound *communication plan* and *timetable.* There can never be too much communication when it comes to a diversity initiative. The first deliverable should be the *business case,* answering the questions, "why are we doing this?"and "what's in it for me?" Success stories need to be communicated frequently. Communication about the diversity initiative is appropriate to both internal and external audiences.

## 2. Shared Vision

The shared vision articulates the organization's definition of diversity and a description of the characteristics of the desired future state of the organization once the initiative has been announced. To be effective, the vision must be embraced by everyone. Some organizations choose to have the crafting of the vision be a collective experience involving leaders and employees to ensure that the process itself is inclusive and that the perspectives, hopes, needs and values of all are reflected. This strategy can help diffuse any cynicism or resulting resistance. It specifies the milestones to be accomplished.

## 3. Shared Values

The *core values* of the organization (the value proposition) that everyone must understand, be committed to and demonstrate are detailed in the shared values.

## 4. Standards

This component includes the *metrics* that will be used to measure progress. Every element of the initiative must be evaluated and measured. How *accountability* will be integrated into the organization (e.g. development of tools such as diversity plans, etc.) is also addressed. *Data gathering methodologies* (e.g., cultural audit, survey, focus group, benchmarking to identify best practices, etc.) to be implemented early in the initiative to establish a *baseline* are outlined. So are proposed *intervention strategies.* How *recognition* and *bonuses* will be awarded is determined.

## 5. Structure

The organizational framework or *infrastructure* (e.g., diversity champions, diversity council, employee resource groups, etc.) that needs to be in place to support the initiative is identified in this element. Whether a task force will be appointed to oversee the initiative is determined. Questions are answered such as, how will procedural issues as opposed to *systemic issues* be dealt with?

How will diversity awareness be promoted (e.g., diversity curriculum, seminars, speakers, brown bags, cultural celebrations, a diversity resource center, etc.)? How will *employee involvement* be optimized? Will there be a *community outreach* component in the initiative? How is *access* to the organization's decision-makers ensured?

## 6. Systems

*People systems* (e.g., recruitment, training, promotion, performance reviews, succession planning, compensation, etc.) are identified that will need to be reviewed and possibly revamped to ensure that diversity is reflected. Other planned or existing policies and practices (e.g., Mentoring, Fast Track Programs, Flex Schedules, etc.) or benefits (e.g., Work/Life Balance, Wellness, Domestic Partner, Long-Term Care, etc.) are addressed.

## 7. Skills

The *core diversity competencies* that will drive organizational results to achieve business goals and competitive advantage are identified. Skill transfer mechanisms and a *training and education program* are detailed. A diversity curriculum may be identified.

## 8. Style

Expectations, particularly of leaders, to role model *desired behaviors* that promote and sustain an inclusive culture, such as trust, respect, dignity, integrity and collaboration, are identified and addressed. Training recommendations required to practice behaviors are included.

## 9. Staff

This element identifies *resources* needed to manage the overall initiative for the organization. For example, decisions as to how many full-time diversity staff professionals will be required and/or whether a diversity leader position will be created are made. *Budget* to implement and sustain the effort is addressed.

Residence  Politics  Family Structure

Union Affiliation  Habits  Organizational Level

Family Status  Education  Birth Order  Communication Style

Ethnicity  Sexual Orientation  Job Function  Work Experience

Age/Generation  Marital Status  Recreational Activities  Personality

# DIMENSIONS OF DIVERSITY

First Language  Race/Color  Religious Beliefs  Learning Style

Appearance  Income  Diversity of Thought  National Origin

Geographic Origin  Job Title  Size  Military Experience

Gender  Tenure  Location  Work Style  Dress

Socio-Economic Status  Mental/Physical Ability

**DIVERSITY**: creating an inclusive culture where differences are sought out and embraced by an organization that is committed to optimizing the potential and contributions of all its employees through trust, respect and empowerment

# COMPONENTS OF A DIVERSITY INITIATIVE

In a 1995 study by the Conference Board of over 50 leading-edge multinational U.S. corporations, some of the following inventory of activities were suggested by representatives from the companies involved as particularly helpful in implementing their diversity initiatives.[125] I have included additional recommendations based on my work in architecting diversity initiative strategies.

## COMMUNICATION

The importance of a well-thought out, strategic communication plan cannot be overstated. Communication vehicles, like those listed below, must be integrated to ensure that messages are consistent and aligned. Nothing can derail a diversity initiative quicker than contradictory information. Leadership credibility is tested, and trust and support risked when communication lacks cohesion and relevance. Many companies are including diversity specialists in their public relations department for this reason.

There are several communication vehicles that are crucial to supporting a diversity initiative.

Given the changing demographics and increasing number of diverse shareholders, customers, suppliers and existing and potential employees, a corporate diversity *mission statement* is critical to articulating a company's commitment to inclusion.

A company's *website* is sometimes the only interface with applicants and potential consumers and investors. Yet, many companies are negligent in articulating their diversity commitment on their websites. Some bury the information on diversity, making it practically inaccessible. Others restrict diversity coverage to the employment or careers section of the website. The most appealing websites are those that have a stand-alone section on diversity.

Diverse constituencies look to websites for evidence of commitment. They want to see how the company is creating opportunity for people of color and women in recruitment, development, promotion and retention practices. They want evidence that diversity populates the ranks, especially senior leadership roles. They look for information on what the company is doing in the public sector to support communities in which they operate. These constituencies are interested in the company's commitment to supporting diversity procurement and courting diverse markets. A good example of an excellent corporate diversity website is *IBM's* (www.empl.ibm.com/diverse).

## INTERNAL COMMUNICATION VEHICLES

- Speeches by CEO/Senior Executives
- Video by CEO
- Teleconferencing
- Communication Meetings
- Department Meetings
- Closed Circuit Television
- Executive Forum
- Corporate Vision Statement
- Diversity Mission Statement
- Diversity Policy
- Diversity Letter/Memo from CEO
- Senior Management Behavior Modeling
- Employee Handbook
- Employee Newspaper/Periodical Articles
- Special Diversity Newsletters/Status Reports
- Second Language Communications
- New Employee Orientation
- New Manager Orientation

## EXTERNAL COMMUNICATION VEHICLES

- Newspaper/Periodical/Internet Articles
- Radio and Television Coverage
- Annual Report
- Participation on Community & National Boards/Task Forces
- Speaking Opportunities at Conferences/Symposia
- National Award Recognition

- Newsletters to Customers, Suppliers, Stakeholders
- Corporate Website
- Diversity Brochure

## EDUCATION AND TRAINING

- Workshops/Lectures/Seminars
- Diversity Briefings for Senior Management
- Diversity Integrated into Executive Education
- Board of Trustees Orientation
- Required Core Courses/Awareness Training
  ○ For Managers
  ○ For Employees
- Sexual Harassment Training
- New Manager Training
- Mainstreaming Diversity into Other Training
- Global Training: Cultural Competence/Global Intelligence
- Train-the-Trainer Programs
- Change Agent Seminars
- Cross Race/Gender Training Teams
- Cross-cultural Communication Training
- Empowerment & Team Effectiveness Training
- Global Cross-cultural Training

## EMPLOYEE INVOLVEMENT

- Task Forces or Teams
- Issue Study Groups
- Focus Groups
- Diversity Council
- Diversity Champion
- Corporate Advisory or Steering Committee
- Business Unit Steering Committee
- Networking Groups
- Cultural Celebrations
- Community Outreach/Volunteerism
- Employee Resource Groups

## CAREER DEVELOPMENT AND PLANNING

- Mentoring
- Executive Sponsorship
- Identification Process for "High Potential" Employees
- Succession Planning
- Expanded Job Posting up to V.P. Level
- Career Pathing
- Individual Development Plans
- Executive MBA Programs
- Developmental Assignments
  - Lateral
  - Rotational
  - Special Short-term
  - Task Forces
- Shadowing
- Internships
- Self-development Planning
- Networking Directories
- Developmental Programs for "Nontraditional" Employees
- English as a Second Language Course
- Accent Reduction Class
- Remedial Education/Skill Upgrading

## PERFORMANCE AND ACCOUNTABILITY

- Link Diversity Performance to other Corporate Objectives
- Develop Diversity Performance Measures
  - Quantitative
  - Qualitative
- Incorporate Diversity in Management by Objectives
- Define and Reward Behaviors that Reinforce Diversity
- Monitor and Report Progress Regularly to Senior Management
- Evaluate Business Units' Performance
- Evaluate Managers' Performance
- Evaluate Employees' Performance

- Tie Diversity Performance to:
  - Business Unit Head's Compensation
  - Business Unit's Bonus Pool
  - Individual Incentive Compensation
  - Direct Compensation
  - Other Rewards and Recognition

## CULTURAL CHANGE

- Conduct Internal Diagnostic Studies
  - Glass Ceiling Audit
  - Equity Analysis of Compensation Practices
  - Culture Audits/Assessments
- Incorporate Diversity Items in Employee Attitude Surveys
- Benchmark Other Companies for Best Practices
- Develop Corporate Diversity Strategy
  Several options include:
  - Establish Stand-Alone Initiative
  - Integrate Diversity into Total Quality Strategy
  - Add Diversity Responsibilities to EEO/AA Position
- Emphasize Line Management Ownership
- Adopt Flexible Managerial Style (not "one size fits all")
- Revise Policies/Benefits to Support Inclusion-based Culture

## INTERNAL DEMOGRAPHICS AND METRICS

- Design Pipeline Recruitment Strategy
- Develop/Monitor Organizational Diversity Plan & Scorecard
- Institute Supplier Procurement Strategy
- Implement Customer Survey on Diversity Practices
- Develop Retention Strategy
- Monitor Workforce Representation, Hires, Promotions and Terminations
- Track Internal/External Employee Grievances

# WORK/LIFE BALANCE PROGRAMS

## Child Care

- On or Near-site Child Care Facilities
- On-site Lactation Rooms
- High Chairs in the Cafeterias
- Subsidized at-home Emergency Care for a Sick Child
- Adoption Assistance
- Pre-natal and Parenting Seminars
- Paid Paternity Leave

## Adult Care

- Resource and Referral Services
- Elder Care Assessment and Case Management
- Emergency Adult Care
- Educational Seminars
- Compressed Work-week

## Flex Scheduling

- Job Sharing
- Telecommuting
- Flex Work Options
- Part-time Assignments

## Employee Wellness

- On-site Fitness Center
- Concierge Services
- Educational Seminars (e.g., stress reduction; weight reduction, etc.)
- Employee Assistance Program
- Massage Therapy Services
- Cell Phone/Pagers for Personal Use

## Insurance Options

- Domestic Partner Benefits
- Long-term Care
- Flex (or cafeteria) Benefits

## COMMUNITY/PUBLIC SECTOR INITIATIVES

- Sponsorship of Community Diversity Program(s)
- Partner with Educational Institution(s) in the Community
- Commit Foundation Grants to support Public Sector Initiative(s)
- Participation on Community/National Boards

# STAYING THE COURSE

When the following checklist of issues in the workplace are proactively addressed and continuously monitored, the likelihood of the initiative stalling are reduced. In turn, substantial cost savings to a company and positive impact to the bottom line can be realized. Following are *cost factors* an organization typically encounters as well as enabling strategies that minimize the negative impact of these costs to the bottom line:

**COST FACTOR:**

## RECRUITMENT

**ENABLING STRATEGIES:**

- Retention Management
- Behavioral Interview Training
- Targeted Advertising
- Strategic Recruiting Plan for U.S./Global Regions includes Pipeline Development and Internships
- 5-year Business Strategy includes Staffing
- National Recognition/Diversity Award

**COST FACTOR:**

## RETENTION

**ENABLING STRATEGIES:**

- Corporate Diversity Initiative
- Employee Resource Groups
- Development Programs
  - Mentoring
  - Executive Shadowing
  - Accelerated Development
  - Leadership Training
- Performance Management
- Bonuses tied to Diversity Management
- Diversity-inclusive Succession Plan

**COST FACTORS:**
## PRODUCTIVITY, QUALITY, CREATIVITY

**ENABLING STRATEGIES:**
- Career Development Plans
- Empowerment/Team Effectiveness Training
- Six Sigma/Continuous Improvement Training
- Skills Upgrade Program

**COST FACTORS:**
## ABSENTEEISM, STRESS & HEALTH-RELATED ISSUES, EMPLOYEE CONFLICT

**ENABLING STRATEGIES:**
- Work/Life Programs
- Alternative Work Arrangements
- Conflict Management Skills Training
- Corporate Diversity Policy
- Sexual Harassment Prevention
- EEO Training

**COST FACTOR:**
## AT-RISK BUSINESS ALLIANCES
(Mergers/Acquisitions/Joint Ventures/Suppliers)

**ENABLING STRATEGIES:**
- Diversity Built into HR Scenario Planning
- Diversity Supplier Procurement Program
- Diversity Supplier Award
- Membership, Billion-Dollar Roundtable

**COST FACTOR:**
## LOW MORALE

**ENABLING STRATEGIES:**
- Employee Attitude Surveys
- Cultural Audit
- Focus Groups
- Employee Resource Groups

**COST FACTOR:**
## CUSTOMER SERVICE/SATISFACTION

**ENABLING STRATEGIES:**
- Customer Service Training
- Cultural Competence Training
- Global Intelligence Initiative

**COST FACTOR:**
## COMPANY REPUTATION/PUBLIC IMAGE

**ENABLING STRATEGIES:**
- Community Alliances Identified to Support Underserved Constituencies
- Foundation Funding for School Initiatives/Scholarships
- Budget/Resource Support for Community Diversity-oriented Programs

**COST FACTOR:**
## SHAREHOLDER VALUE

**ENABLING STRATEGIES:**
- Code of Ethics
- Company Mission
- Core Value Proposition based on trust, respect, integrity, inclusion

# APPENDIX II:

# ESTABLISHING A BASELINE

Substituting data for assumptions helps prevent situations in which solutions go in search of problems. When senior executives propose solutions to some problems but key groups of employees want other problems solved first, those solutions have little credibility. A good solution to the wrong problem is hardly a solution at all.

- Ann M. Morrison
  The New Leaders[126]

# MEASURING THE EFFECTIVENESS OF A DIVERSITY INITIATIVE

Possible methodologies that a company can utilize include a cultural assessment questionnaire, focus groups or one-on-one interviews. Cultural assessments or audits tend to be objective, easy to administer and provide more substantive information.

Before embarking on implementing a diversity initiative, administering a cultural audit is recommended to establish a baseline. Thereafter, annual follow-up assessments should be conducted periodically to measure progress. These become your metrics that drive the initiative.

The importance of measuring effectiveness of an initiative was underscored in a 2001 Korn/Ferry survey on diversity initiatives involving corporate executives and professionals in numerous corporations, all people of color. This survey illuminated a common issue for companies implementing diversity initiatives and demonstrates why their effectiveness needs to be evaluated on a regular basis:

> *Executives tend to rate effectiveness of diversity programs higher than do minority professionals.*[127]

While 57% of executives thought that large organizations in general were effective in their diversity initiatives and 74% thought their own organization, in particular, fell in that category; professionals of color saw it differently. Only 38% believed that large organizations had effective diversity initiatives, while only 48% thought their own organization was effective.

Executives tend to understand diversity as programs in place that they, in many cases, have personally sponsored. Employees, on the other hand, understand diversity in terms of results. It is critical, therefore, to periodically check in with employees to understand their expectations and their experiences as a participant in a diversity initiative.

Both groups in this survey agreed that visible commitment from the CEO and senior leadership team was crucial. Both agreed that skills training was important. The two groups agreed that integrating diversity into business initiatives and tying the initiative to the bottom line was important. Both also agreed that executive bonuses tied to diversity goal achievement was effective. However, the survey also pointed out that only 29% of companies utilize bonuses in this way.

They disagreed on which programs were most effective. With regard to hiring, executives believed that relationships with minority-oriented organizations (e.g., National Association for the Advancement of Colored People, National Council of La Raza, etc.) was most important, while professionals felt that strong support of internship programs was. The professionals believed long-term relationships with recruitment firms that specialized in diversity was effective.

There was disagreement as well on some of the "sacred cows" of diversity initiatives: mentoring, affinity groups and diversity councils, with executives tending to give them higher scores than professionals.

Overwhelming research substantiates the need to include these components in a diversity initiative. They are, in my opinion, crucial to the recruitment, advancement and retention of diverse constituencies. Their effectiveness should be measured regularly using a cultural audit.

Benchmarking periodically for best practices is also recommended. A sample of survey questions is provided.

# CULTURAL AUDIT

_____ (Company Name) believes that the guiding principles of respect for the individual and uncompromising integrity are fundamental to a productive, creative and diverse workplace. This survey is designed to assess how effective we are as an organization relative to diversity issues.

## Definition of Diversity

Diversity refers to an individual's or organization's ability to value and utilize differences in others. These differences include ethnicity, gender, age, disability, race and sexual orientation. Diversity also encompasses differences in life and cultural experiences that affect our perspectives, capabilities, values, communication and work styles and the ways in which we learn and problem-solve.

## Confidentiality

Overall results will be shared with the leadership team who will formulate a plan to address issues that surface. No individual results will be released. Your name has been selected on a random basis, and anonymity is assured.

## Instructions

This survey should be answered within the context of your work group. Please answer as honestly as possible. Don't spend a lot of time on each question; rather, go with your first instinct.

# PLEASE SUPPLY THE FOLLOWING DEMOGRAPHIC DATA BY CHECKING THE APPROPRIATE RESPONSE:

Sex:
- ☐ Male
- ☐ Female

Ethnicity:
- ☐ African-American
- ☐ Asian
- ☐ Caucasian
- ☐ Hispanic
- ☐ Native American

Age:
- ☐ 18 - 25
- ☐ 26 -35
- ☐ 36 - 45
- ☐ 46 - 55
- ☐ 56 +

Function:
- ☐ Administrative Support (eg. clerical, secretarial)
- ☐ Engineer
- ☐ Manufacturing Supv/Mgr
- ☐ Manufacturing Support (eg., Customer Svs, Material Handling, Prod Control, Planning, Receiving, QA, Warehouse)
- ☐ Non-Manufacturing Supv/Mgr
- ☐ Non-Engineering Individual Contributor (eg., Finance, HR, IS, Plant Svs, Sales, Supply Management)
- ☐ Production Operator
- ☐ Technician

Organization: (Name):

Education:
- ☐ Less than High School
- ☐ High School Diploma
- ☐ Some College
- ☐ Associates Degree
- ☐ Undergraduate Degree
- ☐ Grad Degree

| Years of Service: | ☐ | 0 - 2 |
| | ☐ | 3 - 5 |
| | ☐ | 6 - 10 |
| | ☐ | 11 - 15 |
| | ☐ | 16 + |

| Shift: | ☐ | 1st |
| | ☐ | 2nd |
| | ☐ | 3rd & 4th |
| | ☐ | week-end |

| Job Grade: | (specifiy): |

## TERMINOLOGY

The term "**minority**" refers to ethnicity and race (eg. individuals who are not Caucasian).

The term "**non-minority**" refers to individuals who are Caucasian.

The term "**supervisor**" refers to your immediate supervisor.

The term "**manager**" refers to managers above your supervisor up to and including most senior leadership.

The term "**organization**" refers to the business group you work in (e.g., Finance).

If you are unsure how to respond to an item using a business group perspective, respond to the item with your immediate work group in mind.

# 1 = Strongly Agree, 2 = Agree, 3 = Disagree, 4 = Strongly Disagree

1. I feel comfortable with people of diverse backgrounds.   1☐  2☐  3☐  4☐

2. There is diversity at all levels of my organization.   1☐  2☐  3☐  4☐

3. Minorities and women are represented at senior levels in my organization.   1☐  2☐  3☐  4☐

4. Jokes and comments about the following subjects are not tolerated in my work area:
   - a.) age   1☐  2☐  3☐  4☐
   - b.) disability   1☐  2☐  3☐  4☐
   - c.) ethnicity or race   1☐  2☐  3☐  4☐
   - d.) gender   1☐  2☐  3☐  4☐
   - e.) sexual orientation   1☐  2☐  3☐  4☐
   - f.) religion   1☐  2☐  3☐  4☐

5. Managers in my organization hold men and women equally accountable.   1☐  2☐  3☐  4☐

6. Women are given fair consideration for promotions within my organization.   1☐  2☐  3☐  4☐

7. Managers in my organization hold minorities and non-minorities equally accountable.   1☐  2☐  3☐  4☐

8. "Unwritten rules" are shared and understood by non-minorities and minorities.   1☐  2☐  3☐  4☐

9. People are treated with respect regardless of their personal characteristics, lifestyle or cultural perspectives in my organization.   1☐  2☐  3☐  4☐

10. In my organization, the opinions of men are considered more credible by leadership than those of women.   1☐  2☐  3☐  4☐

11. Managers in my organization do not treat heterosexual and gay and lesbian employees differently.   1☐  2☐  3☐  4☐

**1 = Strongly Agree, 2 = Agree, 3 = Disagree, 4 = Strongly Disagree**

12. Managers in my organization make an effort to identify the talents and goals of all employees.    1☐ 2☐ 3☐ 4☐

13. I feel there is more than one right way to accomplish work.    1☐ 2☐ 3☐ 4☐

14. In my organization, it is OK for me to express views which differ from the norm.    1☐ 2☐ 3☐ 4☐

15. In my organization, the opinions of non-minorities are considered more credible than minorities.    1☐ 2☐ 3☐ 4☐

16. Members of minority groups feel included in my organization    1☐ 2☐ 3☐ 4☐

17. My supervisor ensures that when teams are formed, diversity is represented.    1☐ 2☐ 3☐ 4☐

18. I believe seeking diverse viewpoints encourages creativity and innovation.    1☐ 2☐ 3☐ 4☐

19. In my organization, heterosexual employees are considered more credible than gay or lesbian employees.    1☐ 2☐ 3☐ 4☐

20. I am aware of my assumptions, stereotypes and paradigms that are a result of my experiences.    1☐ 2☐ 3☐ 4☐

21. Managers in my organization are held accountable for developing awareness and diversity-oriented behaviors within their staffs.    1☐ 2☐ 3☐ 4☐

22. Minorities are given fair consideration for promotions within my organization.    1☐ 2☐ 3☐ 4☐

23. Members of minority groups feel valued in my organization.    1☐ 2☐ 3☐ 4☐

## 1 = Strongly Agree, 2 = Agree, 3 = Disagree, 4 = Strongly Disagree

24. I believe managing diverse teams is worth the effort.   1☐  2☐  3☐  4☐

25. My supervisor encourages confronting inappropriate behaviors.   1☐  2☐  3☐  4☐

26. Policies are flexible enough to accommodate differences with regard to:
   a.) age   1☐  2☐  3☐  4☐
   b.) disability   1☐  2☐  3☐  4☐
   c.) race or ethnicity   1☐  2☐  3☐  4☐
   d.) gender   1☐  2☐  3☐  4☐
   e.) sexual orientation   1☐  2☐  3☐  4☐
   f.) religion   1☐  2☐  3☐  4☐

27. Managers in my organization ensure full involvement of all employees in meetings.   1☐  2☐  3☐  4☐

28. My supervisor ensures that members of minority groups are heard and acknowledged in meetings.   1☐  2☐  3☐  4☐

29. My organization encourages the celebration of diversity.   1☐  2☐  3☐  4☐

30. My supervisor is effective in recognizing culture clashes resulting from differences in:
   a.) age   1☐  2☐  3☐  4☐
   b.) disability   1☐  2☐  3☐  4☐
   c.) race or ethnicity   1☐  2☐  3☐  4☐
   d.) gender   1☐  2☐  3☐  4☐
   e.) sexual orientation   1☐  2☐  3☐  4☐
   f.) religion   1☐  2☐  3☐  4☐

31. I feel there are definite benefits from working in a diverse group.   1☐  2☐  3☐  4☐

32. My manager models behaviors demonstrating a genuine commitment to diversity principles.   1☐  2☐  3☐  4☐

## 1 = Strongly Agree, 2 = Agree, 3 = Disagree, 4 = Strongly Disagree

33. Working toward diversity at all levels in my organization is seen as a strategic advantage.   1☐  2☐  3☐  4☐

34. I understand how diversity can positively impact the business.   1☐  2☐  3☐  4☐

35. In my organization, diversity is viewed as an integral part of our culture.   1☐  2☐  3☐  4☐

36. In my organization, diversity is viewed as a Human Resources program.   1☐  2☐  3☐  4☐

37. I believe valuing differences has a positive impact on the business.   1☐  2☐  3☐  4☐

38. In my organization, it is an advantage to be a non-minority.   1☐  2☐  3☐  4☐

39. I feel that everyone is unique, with differing values and perspectives.   1☐  2☐  3☐  4☐

40. I am perplexed by the culturally different behaviors I see.   1☐  2☐  3☐  4☐

41. I feel that newcomers should adapt to the mainstream culture.   1☐  2☐  3☐  4☐

42. In my organization, gay and lesbian employees can feel safe to reveal their sexual orientation at work.   1☐  2☐  3☐  4☐

43. I believe women are overly sensitive to prejudice and discrimination.   1☐  2☐  3☐  4☐

44. I think immigrants should give up their own culture and accept the mainstream culture.   1☐  2☐  3☐  4☐

45. I believe minorities are overly sensitive to prejudice and discrimination.   1☐  2☐  3☐  4☐

46. I believe diversity brings unnecessary conflict and makes teaming in my organization more difficult.   1☐  2☐  3☐  4☐

## 1 = Strongly Agree, 2 = Agree, 3 = Disagree, 4 = Strongly Disagree

47. I believe people are more motivated to be productive when they feel accepted for who they are.  1☐ 2☐ 3☐ 4☐

48. I am comfortable with the topic of sexual orientation.  1☐ 2☐ 3☐ 4☐

49. I believe people should leave their differences at home and conform to organizational standards at work.  1☐ 2☐ 3☐ 4☐

50. I'm reluctant to disagree with employees of diverse groups for fear of being considered prejudiced.  1☐ 2☐ 3☐ 4☐

51. I know about my own cultural background and how it influences my behavior and my expectations of others.  1☐ 2☐ 3☐ 4☐

52. There are no negative repercussions in my organization for people who are gay or lesbian.  1☐ 2☐ 3☐ 4☐

53. I'm fearful of offending employees of diverse groups by saying the wrong thing.  1☐ 2☐ 3☐ 4☐

54. I know that different cultural values and behaviors may influence my perceptions of a person's competence.  1☐ 2☐ 3☐ 4☐

55. I'm not sure what to call people from diverse groups. (For example, African-American or Black; Asian-American or Oriental; Hispanic or Latino; people of color or minorities).  1☐ 2☐ 3☐ 4☐

56. No employees are left out of social gatherings in my organization.  1☐ 2☐ 3☐ 4☐

57. I get frustrated when communicating with individuals who have heavy accents or limited English-speaking skills.  1☐ 2☐ 3☐ 4☐

# 1 = Strongly Agree, 2 = Agree, 3 = Disagree, 4 = Strongly Disagree

---

58. In my organization, minorities are considered for highly visible jobs just as often as non-minorities.

1 ☐  2 ☐  3 ☐  4 ☐

---

59. When dealing with differences, I am able to "walk in someone else's shoes."

1 ☐  2 ☐  3 ☐  4 ☐

---

60. Women are represented at senior levels in my organization.

1 ☐  2 ☐  3 ☐  4 ☐

---

61. In my organization, minorities receive just as much recognition as non-minorities.

1 ☐  2 ☐  3 ☐  4 ☐

---

62. Having a diverse workforce has lowered our standards of competence.

1 ☐  2 ☐  3 ☐  4 ☐

---

63. In my organization, women are considered for highly visible jobs just as often as men.

1 ☐  2 ☐  3 ☐  4 ☐

---

64. Women receive just as much recognition as men in my organization.

1 ☐  2 ☐  3 ☐  4 ☐

---

65. I find many similarities between me and my diverse coworkers.

1 ☐  2 ☐  3 ☐  4 ☐

---

66. My manager seeks out multicultural perspectives when making decisions.

1 ☐  2 ☐  3 ☐  4 ☐

---

67. My manager works to eliminate cultural bias in hiring practices.

1 ☐  2 ☐  3 ☐  4 ☐

---

68. My supervisor ensures that women are heard and acknowledged in meetings.

1 ☐  2 ☐  3 ☐  4 ☐

---

69. My supervisor supports training and cultural experiences that expand diversity awareness.

1 ☐  2 ☐  3 ☐  4 ☐

---

70. I feel included in the diversity initiative and that my needs are being met.

1 ☐  2 ☐  3 ☐  4 ☐

---

## ADDITIONAL QUESTIONS (OPTIONAL):

### 1 = Strongly Agree, 2 = Agree, 3 = Disagree, 4 = Strongly Disagree

1. I am satisfied with my job.   1☐  2☐  3☐  4☐

2. My management is sensitive to my personal   1☐  2☐  3☐  4☐
   circumstances.

3. Please rate the effectiveness of the following components of our
   diversity initiative: (List components)

| | | |
|---|---|---|
| Mentoring | ☐ Effective | ☐ Needs Improvement |
| Employee Resource Groups | ☐ Effective | ☐ Needs Improvement |
| Diversity Council | ☐ Effective | ☐ Needs Improvement |
| Networking Sessions | ☐ Effective | ☐ Needs Improvement |
| Lunch & Learn Sessions | ☐ Effective | ☐ Needs Improvement |
| Speakers | ☐ Effective | ☐ Needs Improvement |
| Diversity Skills Training | ☐ Effective | ☐ Needs Improvement |
| Etc. | ☐ Effective | ☐ Needs Improvement |

### PLEASE SHARE COMMENTS:

## BENCHMARKING QUESTIONS

It's good business practice to benchmark periodically for best practices. Select the questions that are most appropriate for your organization.

1.  How does your company define diversity to create common understanding?

2.  How long have you had a diversity initiative?

3.  What are the components of the initiative?

4.  Who leads the effort?

5.  What are the key factors in your success?

6.  What are key concerns/obstacles?

7.  What are your metrics?

8.  What is your business case?

9.  What results have you had?

10. Who are your key stakeholders?

11. What are the key roles and their responsibilities in your diversity initiative?

12. What are your key strategies?

13. If your initiative involves a cultural change effort, describe those strategies.

14. What systems/processes do you focus on?

15. What is the infrastructure to support diversity?

16. What dimensions of diversity (eg., gender, ethnicity, age, etc.) does your initiative include?

17. What tools have you utilized/developed that have been most helpful?

18. If you offer a diversity curriculum, please describe. Who attends? How often?

19. Who do you benchmark for best practices?

20. What community outreach efforts have you focused on to increase your company's visibility or recognition around diversity?

21. What sourcing/recruiting strategies have you implemented to attract diverse talent?

22. If your diversity initiative employs retention strategies, please describe.

23. Describe any career development efforts targeting diverse talent you've implemented.

24. If you have a succession planning process, how is diversity included?

25. How do you hold managers accountable for achieving diversity goals?

26. If you can, please share the amount of resources dedicated to your diversity initiative (eg., budget and staff).

27. What are the key competencies and behaviors diverse leaders should command?

28. If your initiative involves your markets and customer base, please describe how.

29. Does your initiative support employee resource groups? What are they and how are they utilized to support the effort?

30. If your diversity initiative includes diversity procurement efforts, please describe.

31. Describe effective strategies you've implemented in your communication/marketing efforts.

32. Who owns your diversity initiative?

33. How do you get employees involved in the process?

34. Please share your key lessons learned in designing/implementing a diversity initiative.

35. Is your diversity initiative global?

---

**(IF YES, CONTINUE WITH FOLLOWING QUESTIONS)**

---

36. What countries/regions participate?

37. How does your company define diversity to create common understanding globally?

38. How did you implement your global strategy?

39. What strategies did you implement to keep the initiative from being U.S.-centric?

40. What are the components of your global diversity initiative? Are they common to all countries/regions?

41. What are your metrics? Do they differ by country/region?

42. Who leads the effort globally? How are they held accountable?

43. If you have a business case for diversity that is global in nature, please describe.

44. What training do you offer globally?

45. What communication strategies/vehicles have you utilized to keep global diversity champions "on the same page?"

# APPENDIX III:

# METRICS

The lack of measurement practices for diversity sets managing and leveraging diversity apart from the rest of the organization. While peers in other organizational areas are focusing on metrics..., those implementing the diversity process may limit its contribution... [by focusing only on] increased awareness. It is a real opportunity missed, [causing diversity to be thought of as] ... a non-business oriented endeavor which contributes little to bottom line performance.

- Edward E. Hubbard, Ph.D.[128]
  Measuring Diversity Results

# METRICS: THE HEART OF THE BUSINESS CASE FOR DIVERSITY

Metrics can be designed to *support key strategies,* give an initiative direction and *objectively evaluate* the effectiveness and results of virtually *every component* of a diversity initiative. Dr. Edward Hubbard's *Diversity 9-S Framework* model provides a basic foundation and methodology for tracking progress and success of diversity initiatives.

Numbers is the language of business. Without numbers to lend direction and credibility to an initiative, no program, especially diversity, will be taken seriously as a contributor to profitability. The chance of diversity being seen as a strategic business imperative is lost. Management support and follow-through is sub-optimized. Without metrics, the basic question remains, how else do you know if you've made progress?

Metrics are at the core of a compelling business case for diversity.

## MEASURING DIVERSITY RESULTS

A diversity effort needs to achieve positive **results** in key areas. And results can be quantified. As Edward Hubbard demonstrates in his resourceful book, *Measuring Diversity Results,* there are many data collection systems and productivity measurement tools that will provide feedback to an organization regarding progress and effectiveness of a particular diversity program.

For example, on the most fundamental level, we can calculate costs of a diversity recruiting program using Dr. Hubbard's formula:

$$\text{Cost per Diversity Hire} = \frac{AC + AF + RB + N\text{-}CH}{\text{Total Diversity Hires}}$$

AC = Advertising Costs
AF = Agency Fees
RB = Referral Bonuses
N-CH = No-Cost Hires

Similarly, diversity attrition can be measured – and by any number of variables: length of service, job grade, job class, performance, etc.

Dr. Hubbard also provides a formula to measure productivity (defined as gross revenue in dollars per employee) shown as a ratio per employee for each year:

$$\text{Productivity} = \frac{\text{Yr 1 Revenues + Yr 2 Revenues + Yr 3 Revenues}}{\text{Average \# Employees}}$$

On a more complex level, we can actually measure ROI. Following is Hubbard's example of calculating a 40% return on investment for a work/life training program:

Initial Cost: . . . . . . . . . . . . . . . . $50,000
Shelf Life of Program: . . . . . . . . 3 years
Residual Value after 3 years: . . . . 0
Net Savings/Year: . . . . . . . . . . . $10,000 ($30,000/3)
Average Investment/Year: . . . . . . $25,000 (ave. book value = 1/2 cost)

$$\text{Average ROI} \quad = \quad \frac{\text{annual savings}}{\text{average investment}}$$

$$= \quad \frac{\$10,000}{\$25,000}$$

$$= \quad 40\%$$

Marketing plans targeting advertising to various ethnic multicultural customer bases lend themselves just as well to such an ROI metric. So do sales campaigns.

Creating "early warning" systems and tracking and reporting metrics on a regular basis are key to the success of a diversity initiative.

# AN INVENTORY OF METRICS

Establishing metrics is not difficult. The following is a sample menu of the possibilities:

## Internal Demographics

- # Hires
- # Promotions
- # Terminations
- # Absentees by department
- # Returns from Leave
- % Current Workforce Representation by Group
  (eg., by race and gender; by total; by department)
- % Change of Above Indices/Group/Period of Time
- % Goal Attainment
- $ Cost per Hire
- # Referrals by Source
- # Offers vs. Interviews
- # Offers Made vs. Accepts
- % Hired vs. Applicant Flow
- % Favorable Responses Applicant Survey
- % Promoted vs. Pipeline Incumbents
- % Promotion-ready Candidates, year to year
- # Years Average Tenure by Diverse Group
- # Hires Correlated to Performance Level
- # Results of Compensation/Equity Analysis and Actions Taken
- # External Charges/# Internal Grievances
  (eg., by total; by department)
- $ Costs of Litigation (eg., external charges, lawsuits, settlements, legal fees)

## Employee Satisfaction

- % Favorable Responses in Employee Survey or Cultural Audit
- # Responses/Factor on Exit Interview
- % Utilization of Work/Life Program
- % Absenteeism/Group/Time Frame
- # Complaints/Grievances/Lawsuits

## Career Development

- % Positions filled from Succession Plan
- # Development Plans Completed/Business Unit
- # Performance Evaluations Completed/Business Unit
- % Mentoring Assignments Filled
- % High Potentials/Business Unit
- % Promotion-ready Diversity Candidates

## Training

- % Diversity Training Completed
- % Change in Comparison/Pre- and Post Workshop
- % Change Diversity Attitude/Pre- and Post
- % Change Diversity Competencies/Pre- and Post

## Components of Diversity Initiative

- # Diversity Teams/Business Unit
- % Budget Allocated to Diversity
- % Favorable Responses from Employee Resource Group Survey
- % Change in Retention/Time Frame
- # Times Diversity Mentioned as Strategy in Business Goal Accomplishment
- # Times Diversity Vision/Mission/Strategy Mentioned
- # People Systems/Policies Assessed for Diversity Impact
- # People Systems/Policies Updated for Diversity Impact

- # Organizational Diversity Plans Completed
- % Managers Receiving Bonus for Effective Diversity Management
- # Diversity Components Implemented due to Benchmarking
- # Focus Groups/One-on-One Interviews Conducted, Results and Actions Taken

## External Demographics

- # Recognition Awards for Diversity Initiative
- % Change Customer Demographics/Domestic/Global
- % Change New Customer Base/Domestic/Global
- % Change Market Share/Domestic/Global
- % Favorable Customer Survey
- % Change Diversity Suppliers
- % Budget Diversity Procurement
- % Budget Foundation Grants Supporting Public Sector Initiatives
- # Sponsored Community Events
- # Employees Involved in Supporting Community Initiatives
- # Scholarships Awarded
- # National/Community Board Positions Filled
- % Workforce Representation of Current/Projected Customer Base by race, gender
- % Comparison of Your Workforce vs. Customer Workforce
- # Countries/Cultures/Languages by Customer vs. Your Workforce Representation
- % Composition of Leadership of Customer vs. Your Leadership Representation
- # Customer Complaints by Issue
- % Comparison of Customer Complaints Current Year vs. Past Year
- $ Loss of Customers

# ORGANIZATIONAL DIVERSITY SCORECARD

Diversity scorecards are developed by each group within a company to guide diversity achievement across the organization. This tool helps groups track progress and stay the course. It is also an effective approach to ensuring that all groups within an organization are "on the same page" in meeting the stated diversity objectives of the overall organization. Scorecards should be prepared annually and monitored, updated and reported on quarterly. They include a wide range of actions and goals, examples of which follow.

People throughout the organization are needed to execute on the scorecard. Providing an opportunity for employees to assist the organization in achieving progress on the scorecard gives them a role as change agent. They then can contribute to developing proactive strategies that address issues concerning them and their colleagues, which helps them acquire new skills and gives them visibility to higher levels of management. This involvement is critical in motivating and retaining employees.

# ORGANIZATIONAL DIVERSITY SCORECARD
## (Example)

**DIVERSITY INITIATIVE COMPONENT:**

CULTURE & ENVIRONMENT

**STRATEGIES:**

- Complete Cultural Audit & Follow-Up
- Benchmark for Best Practices

**DIVERSITY INITIATIVE COMPONENT:**

LEADERSHIP COMMITMENT

**STRATEGIES:**

- Include Diversity Topic in Communication Meetings
- Sponsor Diversity Speaker each Quarter
- Attend National Diversity Conference

**DIVERSITY INITIATIVE COMPONENT:**

PEOPLE SYSTEMS

**STRATEGIES:**

- Ensure Diversity Candidates Included in Succession Plan
- Conduct follow-up Interviews on all Voluntary Terminations & Track Reasons
- Ensure 100% Completion of Performance Evaluations/ Career Discussions

**DIVERSITY INITIATIVE COMPONENT:**

ORGANIZATIONAL EFFECTIVENESS

**STRATEGIES:**

- Develop Annual Communication Plan
- Allocate Budget

- Develop Annual Calendar for Diversity Council
- Identify/Assign Resources (e.g., Champions, Executive Sponsors, Team Leaders)

**DIVERSITY INITIATIVE COMPONENT:**
PEOPLE DEVELOPMENT

**STRATEGIES:**

- Design Mentoring Program & Implement
- Ensure Senior Leadership Members Achieve Mentorship Goals of Women and People of Color
- Identify Key Talent & Develop Leadership Experiences for Them

**DIVERSITY INITIATIVE COMPONENT:**
WORKFORCE PLANNING, SOURCING & RECRUITMENT

**STRATEGIES:**

- Set Goals/Develop Plan for InternshipProgram
- Participate in National/Regional Diversity Conferences/Job Fairs
- Complete Annual Workforce Plan & Establish Diversity Goals

**DIVERSITY INITIATIVE COMPONENT:**
TRAINING (Skills, Knowledge, Behaviors)

**STRATEGIES:**

- Ensure all Employees attend at least one Diversity Class

**DIVERSITY INITIATIVE COMPONENT:**
EDUCATION (Awareness)

**STRATEGIES:**

- Schedule Global Intelligence/Cultural Competence Workshop for Leaders

**DIVERSITY INITIATIVE COMPONENT:**
## EMPLOYEE INVOLVEMENT

**STRATEGIES:**
- Support Employee Participation in Lunch & Learn Sessions
- Ensure Leadership Sponsorship for Diversity Team Leaders & Champions

**DIVERSITY INITIATIVE COMPONENT:**
## COMMUNITY OUTREACH

**STRATEGIES:**
- Host at least one Diversity-related Community Event
- Encourage/Track Participation on Boards

**DIVERSITY INITIATIVE COMPONENT:**
## EXTERNAL EDUCATIONAL INITIATIVES

**STRATEGIES:**
- Select one High School to Mentor/Support Fully for the Year
- Sponsor Internships for High School Seniors
- Sponsor at least one College Scholarship

**DIVERSITY INITIATIVE COMPONENT:**
## GOALS & METRICS

**STRATEGIES:**
- Increase Staff Diversity by $\underline{X}$ %
- Achieve Hiring/Promotion Goals
- Design Leadership Bonus Program & Monitor Diversity Achievement
- Monitor & Reduce Turnover

# APPENDIX IV:

# INCLUSION-BASED LEADERSHIP COMPETENCIES

Cultural Diversity in the global market must be recognized not simply as a fact of life, but as a positive benefit ... Cultural competence must be recognized as a key management skill.

- O'Hara-Devereaux and Johansen
  GlobalWork[129]

# DESIRED SKILLSET & BEHAVIORS

Culturally competent leaders are *courageous pioneers* who are *catalysts for change, inspiring visionaries* and *evangelists "of the heart"* who *care about people, encourage excellence,* believe in *lifelong learning* and work to *remove the barriers to inclusion and equity.*

Following is a catalog of leadership competencies desirable in a company committed to inclusion, both in the U.S. and globally:

## Foundational Competencies

* Language Fluency
* Global Cultural Intelligence
  (including a grounding in one's own culture)
  ○ Cross-cultural Communication Skills
  ○ Cross-cultural Mentoring Skills
  ○ Cross-cultural Coaching & Performance Feedback Skills
  ○ Cross-cultural Interviewing Skills
  ○ Cross-cultural Conflict Resolution Skills
* Facilitation
* Management by Empowerment
  (Participative Decision-Making; Decentralized)
* Problem-solving; Listening; Input/Feedback Solicitation
* Technology Literacy
* Systems Thinking
* Ability to Function as a World Citizen
  ○ Global Acumen (Living in/Experiencing Other Cultures)
  ○ Knowledge of International Relations, Foreign Affairs, Government, History, Customs, Beliefs
* Effective, Open & Flexible Communication Style that Facilitates Clarity in Cross-cultural Dialogue

- Orientation to Developing/Strengthening Others
- Ability to Build/Sustain Global Coalitions, Teams & Collaborators
- Opportunistic in Creating Recognition/Celebrating Accomplishments
- Shares Information/Shares Power
- Orientation to Challenging the Process/Continuous Improvement
- Scenario-Planning

## Behaviors that Support Inclusion

- Listens/Seeks first to Understand and then Be Understood
- Demonstrates On-going Awareness of Personal Biases & Stereotypes
- Commits to Examining/Understanding Own Attitudes & Behaviors and those of Other Cultures
- Articulates Business Case for Diversity
- Treats Everyone with Respect, Dignity and Cultural Sensitivity
- Builds Trust & Collaborative Relationships
- Challenges Inappropriate Language & Behavior
- Works to Eliminate Cultural Bias in Hiring, Performance Standards & Barriers to Advancement
- Recognizes/Constructively Manages the Dynamics of Prejudice in Group Interactions
- Provides Support to Others in Overcoming Language/Cultural Barriers
- Gives Accurate, Objective Feedback to Employees & Takes Appropriate Action when Expectations are not Met
- Expects Accountability for Diversity from Managers in his/her Organization
- Manages/Distributes Rewards for Results
- Seeks out/Incorporates/Acknowledges Multicultural Perspectives & Approaches in Decision-Making
- Supports Diversity-enabling Initiatives (e.g., Employee Resource Groups; Alternative Work Schedules; Work/Life Balance; Accelerated Development Programs; Targeted Recruitment; Domestic Partner Benefits, etc.)

- Participates in Training & Cultural Experiences that Expand Awareness
- Is Entrepreneurial
- Is a Risk-Taker & Able to Live with Failure
- Has a Sense of Humor
- Is both Patient and Curious

# INVENTORY OF KEY LEADERSHIP EXPERIENCES

Creating developmental opportunities for women and people of color is critical in providing them visibility and experiences necessary to qualify for higher positions of increasing responsibility. Below is a checklist of just some of the key leadership experiences an organization might consider as a part of a development plan.

1. Attend Technical Conference/Symposium

2. Participate in Executive Development Initiative

3. Participate in Rotation or Cross-training Program, Domestic and Global

4. Accompany a Senior Level Executive on Customer Visit, Global and Domestic

5. Accompany a Senior Level Executive on Supplier Visit, Global and Domestic

6. Attend Staff Meeting, Group Staff Meeting and Operations Review within and outside of Organization

7. Attend Worldwide Strategy Meeting

8. Visit Sales Office. Spend a week Shadowing Staff.

9. Publish Technical Paper

10. Volunteer for a Special Assignment, such as:
    - Champion a Supplier
    - Conduct Research for Organization/Benchmark; Prepare Final Report and Present to Staff
    - Lead a Task Force, Domestic or Global
    - Take a Short-term Assignment Overseas or with a Different Business
    - Act as Liaison between Organizations having Difficulties Teaming; Recommend Corrective Action

11. Serve on a Community Board

12. Identify Mentor(s) within and outside of Organization; Meet Regularly

13. Become a Coach for a New Hire

14. Participate in Recruitment Activity and on Interview Team
15. Participate in Informal Networking Events with Managers and Peers
16. Enroll in Leadership and Diversity Training
17. Become an Officer in a Professional Society/Organization
18. Shadow an Executive
19. Read Books/Articles in Accordance with Development Plan
20. Attend Graduate School
21. Learn Second Language
22. Complete in-basket Exercise and Review Process with Manager
23. Lead a Community Drive for your Organization (e.g. United Way)
24. Serve as an Advisor to a Non-Profit Organization
25. Teach a Class

# APPENDIX V:

# DIVERSITY RECRUITMENT & SOURCING STRATEGIES

Employment criteria are too often based on assumptions about what is needed to perform the job, and they often exclude - by design or accident - nontraditional candidates who lack the credentials or previous experience historically included as requirements.

- Ann Morrison
  The New Leaders[130]

# DIVERSITY RECRUITMENT STRATEGIES

Once a company is hiring, how can it optimize its opportunity to acquire diverse talent? Following are some success criteria that will aid in the process:

1. When a job requisition is approved, ensure that the requirements are really the ones needed to do the job, not presumed qualifications based on historical assumptions. A too narrow or too vague job description restricts the pool of candidates, often eliminating diverse candidates from consideration.

2. The job needs to be a "real" job with substance, responsibility and opportunities for advancement. Consciously or unconsciously, some organizations identify certain "niche" jobs for diverse candidates or end up creating jobs. In either case, the candidate's potential will be restricted, performance expectations will remain low and he or she could be made to feel exploited.

3. Recruiters, hiring managers and interview teams need to be properly trained on effective and objective screening and interviewing processes. Companies that have adopted structured behavioral-based interviewing (as advocated by expert Bradford Smart in his must-read book, *Topgrading*) can reduce the effects of beliefs, attitudes and stereotyping that contribute to subjective, sometimes biased, candidate evaluation.

   Depending on the level of public and demonstrated commitment a company has to a diversity initiative, it goes without saying that recruiters and hiring teams need to be well-versed in the components of the initiative. They need to anticipate direct, sometimes difficult, questions (e.g., how does your company's commitment to diversity play out in your organization? What is the typical timeframe for promotions for someone of my background?). Recruiters and hiring teams also need to feel comfortable talking openly to diverse candidates about perceived barriers as well as opportunities.

Equally important is a hiring team's knowledge about the business case for diversity. Hiring diverse talent contributes to enriching the company's portfolio of ideas (e.g., potential future patents) and problem-solving capabilities. A diverse workforce helps to attract a diverse customer base, enabling a company to achieve competitive advantage and generate greater profits. In many organizations the impact of hiring the right people on potential profit remains disconnected. Individuals involved in the hiring process need to demonstrate comfort and skill in dealing with cultural differences, being particularly sensitive to various preferred communication styles.

4.  Hiring team members need to reflect diversity. This should be a standard practice, not just when a diverse candidate is being interviewed. Ensure the candidate has ample opportunity to talk with "people like them" that are from all levels of the organization. When recruiting on campus or at job fairs, ensure that the team reflects diversity. If the job fair or conference is sponsored by a diversity organization, sending a diverse recruiting team gives the message that the company really is interested in diversity. Not doing so sends exactly the opposite message. When campus recruiting, ensure that you send diverse recruiters to speak to diversity organizations (e.g., NSBE, SWE, SHPE, MAES, NSHMBA and NBMBA chapters)[131].

5.  The selection process and offer decision should be swift. When the process takes too long, several outcomes can occur, neither very positive. The diverse candidate can feel compromised, less wanted and less enthusiastic about joining the company - especially if he or she has heard through the grapevine that the process does not take as long for non-diverse candidates. Or, an even likelier scenario - the candidate will become the newest employee of your competitor.

6.  Include information on the community, special programs and upcoming events that might be of interest to a diverse candidate. Customize the packet to the candidate's diversity, where possible.

7.  Strike what Dr. Denise Rousseau of Carnegie Mellon calls "idiosyncratic deals," which include customized job descriptions and conditions of employment tailored to what the highly desired employee is seeking. Towers Perrin, in their 2001 Talent Report, agrees that using discretionary efforts as a way of capturing top performers and retaining them, works.

8.  The war for talent means that every interview is critical. Diversity candidates usually have more than one offer. Treat every candidate as you would a customer. Sell your company, sell your organization, and sell the job. Describe how this job fits into the overall scheme of the organization. Be prepared to discuss job progression and likely next assignments. You need to convince the candidate that you are the employer of choice.

9.  Finally, remember that effective talent management, especially hiring, is all about relationship-building with local, regional and national organizations over the long-term, developing a talent pipeline based on trust and investment of time and effort. Hiring should be viewed as a continuous process, not just when a requisition gets approved. Once the war for talent heats up again, the challenge will be for companies to develop effective diversity sourcing strategies, especially ones that focus on the more elusive, passive candidates. Success depends on long-term relationship-building.

# DIVERSITY SOURCING STRATEGIES

A well-conceived, comprehensive diversity sourcing strategy is crucial not only to attracting a top-notch pipeline of nontraditional talent but in establishing a reputation for excellence as a company committed to an inclusion-based culture. A well-defined sourcing strategy will also create operating efficiencies and potential cost savings for the company as it engages in recruitment. A sourcing strategy should include both traditional and non-traditional approaches.

## Traditional Approaches

- Attending *national diversity conferences and career fairs.* Adopt an aggressive presence at these events by including hiring managers on the team to conduct on-the-spot interviews and offers. Distribute marketing literature on your company's diversity initiative, including the vision, goals and strategies. Collect business cards and obtain event attendee lists, then follow-up quickly. These are potential candidates now and in the future.

  Don't miss the opportunity to attend *local and regional events* as they are often less costly and frequently attract candidates who do not require relocation.

- Developing a *multimedia advertising strategy,* which could include print, radio, billboard, direct mailings and Internet job postings. There are literally hundreds of job posting websites that specialize in targeting diverse talent. As a note of caution, however, there is no evidence in the research that suggests diverse candidates are more inclined to use these websites over the "monster.coms" of the world. Nevertheless, *Internet recruiting* can often be the most cost effective of all advertising strategies.

  Using electronic *job boards* that are maintained by professional diversity organizations, such as National Society of Black Engineers or National Black MBA Organization, can be effective.

- Employing *search firms,* including those that specialize in diversity talent. However, as with diversity websites, the same caution applies: there is no evidence to support that diverse candidates are more likely to use search firms that specialize in diversity.

- Utilizing *internal referrals.* Good people know good people. If your company or organization has diversity teams or employee resource groups, approach them about becoming a recruiting resource. This holds true for diverse leaders in your organization.

- Seeking *external referrals.* Community groups, churches, professional associations and customers are all excellent sources for diverse candidates.

- Developing relationships with Historically Black Colleges and Universities (*HBCUs)* and other colleges and universities that have high enrollments of women and people of color in disciplines you are seeking. *Intern programs* are a critical component of a diversity talent pipeline strategy. The *Inroads Program* is an excellent resource for interns of color.

An effective diversity sourcing strategy also needs to include non-traditional, out-of-the-box tactics.

## Non-traditional Approaches

- Hosting *special events* such as *free seminars, open houses and networking sessions,* targeting diversity-oriented community organizations. In today's market, job seekers are looking for every opportunity to network.

- Accessing resume *databases of outplacement firms.* Many of the companies that have experienced downsizing offer outplacement services to their displaced employees.

- Networking with *previous employees* who left your company in good standing. A "boomerang" (e.g., rehire) walking the halls is one of the best advertising and retention strategies you can utilize.

- Establishing contact with former *diverse candidates who were not selected* for employment at the time, but were good candidates, nevertheless. The requirements for the current position might provide a better fit.

- Utilizing non-traditional strategies to target a diverse talent pool such as *virtual job fairs, video interviewing and chat rooms* hosted by diversity websites.

- Incorporating into the orientation process *recommendations from diverse new hires* for names of friends and family members as potential future recruits.

- Following up on *references* diverse candidates have cited on resumes and/or applications.

- Expanding the list of targeted diversity colleges and universities (e.g., include *African and Afro-Caribbean colleges and universities* in your keyword searches).

# APPENDIX VI:

# RECOMMENDED RESOURCES

Our success as a global company is a direct result of our diverse and talented workforce. Our ability to develop new consumer insights and ideas and to execute in a superior way across the world is the best possible testimony to the power of diversity any organization could ever have.

> \- John Pepper, Past CEO[132]
> Proctor & Gamble

# RECOMMENDED RESOURCES

## Books

Althen, Gary, *American Ways: A Guide for Foreigners in the United States*, 2nd ed., (Yarmouth, ME: Intercultural Press, 2002).

Axtell, Roger E., editor, *Do's and Taboos Around the World*, 3rd ed., (White Plains, New York: The Benjamin Company, 1993).

Baytos, Lawrence M., *Designing & Implementing Successful Diversity Programs* (Englewood Cliffs, NJ: Prentice Hall,1995).

Blank, Renee and Sandra Sipp, V*oices of Diversity: Real People Talk About Problems and Solutions in a Workplace Where Everyone is Not Alike* (New York: AMACOM,1994).

Chang, Richard Y., *Capitalizing on Workplace Diversity* (San Francisco, CA: Richard Chang Assoc., 1999).

Cose, Ellis, *The Rage of a Privileged Class* (New York: Harper Collins, 1993).

Covey, Stephen R., *Principle Centered Leadership* (New York: Summit Books,1991).

_____, *Seven Habits of Highly Effective People* (New York: Simon & Schuster, 1989).

Cox, Taylor, *Developing Competency for Managing Diversity* (San Francisco, CA: Berrett-Koehler, 1997).

Cross, Elsie Y. et.al., editors, *The Promise of Diversity* (Burr Ridge, ILL: Irwin Professional Publishing, 1994).

Estess, Patricia Schiff, *Work Concepts for the Future* (Menlo Park, CA: Crisp Publications, 1996).

Gardenswartz, Lee and Anita Rowe, *Diverse Teams at Work: Capitalizing on the Power of Diversity* (Chicago, IL: Irwin Professional Publishing, 1994).

_____, *Managing Diversity: A Complete Desk Reference And Planning Guide* (San Diego, CA: Pfeiffer, 1993).

Graham, L., *Proversity* (New York: John Wiley & Son, 1996).

Griggs, Lewis and Lente-Louise Louw, ed., *Valuing Diversity: New Tools for a New Reality* (New York: McGraw-Hill, 1994).

Guillory, Bill and Linda Galindo, *Empowerment for High-Performing Organizations* (Salt Lake City, UT: Innovations International, 1994).

Hacker, Andrew, *Two Nations: Black and White, Separate, Hostile, Unequal* (New York: Ballantine, 1992).

Hall, Edward, *Understanding Cultural Differences* (Yarmouth, ME: Intercultural Press,1990).

Hampden-Turner, Charles and Fons Trompenaars, *The 7 Cultures of Capitalism* (New York: Currency Doubleday, 1993).

Harris, Philip R. and Robert T. Moran, *Managing Cultural Differences,* 3rd ed., (Houston, TX: Gulf Publishing, 1991).

*Harvard Review on Managing Diversity* (Boston, MA: Harvard Business School, 2002).

Hayles, V. Robert, *The Diversity Directive: Why Some Initiatives Fail and What to Do About It* (New York: McGraw-Hill, 1996).

Hofstede, Geert, *Culture's Consequences: Comparing Values, Behaviors, Institutions and Organizations Across Nations* (Thousand Oaks, CA: Sage Publications, 2001).

_____, *Cultures and Organizations, The Software of the Mind* (New York: McGraw-Hill, 1991).

Hubbard, Edward E., *How to Calculate Diversity Return on Investment* (Petaluma, CA: Global Insights Publishing, 1999).

_____, *Measuring Diversity Results,* Volume 1 (Petaluma, CA: Global Insights Publishing, 1997).

Ipsaro, Anthony J., *White Men, Women & Minorities in the Changing Work Force* (Denver, CO: Meridian Associates, 1997).

Ismail, Luby and Alex Kronemer, *Finding Diversity: A Directory of Recruiting Resources* (SHRM: 2002).

Jamieson, David and Julie O'Mara, *Managing Workforce 2000: Gaining the Diversity Advantage* (San Francisco, CA: Jossey-Bass, 1991).

Johnson, Barry, *Polarity Management: Identifying and Managing Unsolvable Problems* (Amherst, MA: HRD Press, 1996).

Kanter, R.M., *The Challenge of Organizational Change* (New York: Maxwell MacMillan, 1992).

_____, *The Change Masters: Innovations and Entrepreneurship in the American Corporation* (New York: Touchstone, 1985).

Katz, Judith, *White Awareness: Handbook for Anti-Racism Training* (Norman, OK: University of Oklahoma Press, 1978).

Kidder, Rushworth M., *Shared Values for a Troubled World* (San Francisco, CA: Jossey-Bass, 1994).

Kim, Eun Y., *The Yin and Yang of American Culture: A Paradox* (Yarmouth, ME: Intercultural Press, 2001).

Kivel, Paul, *Uprooting Racism: How White People Can Work for Racial Justice* (Philadelphia, PA: New Society Publishers, 1995).

Knouse, Stephen B., Paul Rosenfeld, and Amy Culbertson, eds., *Hispanics in the Workplace* (Newbury Park, CA: Sage Publications, 1984).

Kochman, Thomas, *Black and White Styles in Conflict* (Chicago, ILL: The University Of Chicago Press, 1981).

Kouzes, James M. and Barry Z. Pozner, *The Leadership Challenge: How to Get Extraordinary Things Done in Organizations* (San Francisco, CA: Jossey-Bass,1987).

Kozol, Jonathan, *Savage Inequalities: Children in America's Schools* (New York: Harper Collins, 1991).

Lester, Joan Steinau, *The Future of White Men & Other Diversity Dilemmas* (Berkeley, CA: Conari Press, 1994).

Loden, Marilyn and J.B. Rosener, *Workforce America! Managing Employee Diversity As a Vital Resource* (Homewood, IL: Business One Irwin, 1991).

Loden, Marilyn, *Implementing Diversity* (New York: McGraw-Hill, 1995).

Marinelli, R.P., and A.D. Orto, *The Psychological and Social Impact of Disability* (New York: Springer Publishing, 1991).

McNaught, Brian, *Gay Issues in the Workplace* (New York: St. Martin's Press, 1993).

Miller, Frederick and Judith Katz, *Inclusion Breakthrough:Unleashing the Real Power of Diversity* (San Francisco, CA: Berrett-Koehler, 2002).

Morrison, Ann M., *The New Leaders: Guidelines on Leadership Diversity in America* (San Francisco, CA: Jossey-Bass, 1992).

_____, Randall P. White, and Ellen van Velson, *Breaking the Glass Ceiling* (Reading, MA: Addison-Wesley, 1987).

Morrison, Terri et.al., *Kiss, Bow or Shake Hands: How to Do Business in Sixty Countries* (Holbrook, MA: B. Adams, 1994).

O'Hara-Devereaux and Robert Johansen, *GlobalWork: Bridging Distance, Culture & Time* (San Francisco, CA: Jossey-Bass, 1995).

Palmore, E., *Ageism: Negative and Positive* (New York: Springer Publishing, 1990).

Pharr, Suzanne, *Homophobia: A Weapon of Sexism* (Little Rock, AR: Chardon Press, 1988).

Rose, P. I., *They and We: Racial and Ethnic Relations in the United States,* 4th ed., (New York: McGraw-Hill, 1990).

Rosen, Robert et.al., *Global Literacies: The New Leadership Language for 21st Century Business* (New York: Simon & Schuster, 2000).

Rosenberg, Marshall, B., *Nonviolent Communication: A Language of Compassion* (Encinitas, CA: Puddle Dancer Press, 2000).

Russell, Armida and V. Robert Hayles, *The Diversity Directive: Why Some Initiatives Fail & What to Do About It* (Burr Ridge, IL: Irwin, 1997).

Schein, E.H., *Organizational Culture and Leadership* (San Francisco, CA: Jossey-Bass, 1991).

Smart, Bradford, *Topgrading: How Leading Companies Win by Hiring, Coaching, and Keeping the Best People* (Paramus, NJ: Prentice Hall, 1999).

Stewart, Edward C. and Milton J. Bennett, *American Cultural Patterns: A Cross-Cultural Perspective* (Yarmouth, ME: Intercultural Press, 1991).

Storti, Craig, *The Art of Crossing Cultures* (Yarmouth, ME: Intercultural Press, 1990).

Takaki, Ronald, *A Different Mirror: A History of Multi-cultural America* (Boston, MA: Little Brown, 1993).

Tannen, Deborah, *Talking from 9 to 5* (New York: William Morrow, 1994).

_____, *You Just Don't Understand* (New York: Ballantine Books, 1990).

Thomas, R. Roosevelt and Marjorie Woodruff, *Building a House for Diversity: How a Fable about a Giraffe & Elephant Offers New Strategies for Today's Workforce* (New York: AMACOM, 1999).

_____, *Redefining Diversity* (New York: AMACOM, 1996).

_____, *Beyond Race and Gender: Unleasing the Power of Your Total Work Force by Managing Diversity* (New York: AMACOM, 1991).

Thomas, David A. and John J. Gabarro, *Breaking Through: The Making of Minority Executives in Corporate America* (Boston, MA: Harvard Business School, 1999).

Thiederman, Sondra, *Bridging Cultural Barriers for Corporate Success: How to Manage The Multicultural Work Force* (New York: Free Press, 1990).

Trompenaars, Fons, *Riding the Waves of Culture: Understanding Cultural Diversity in Business* (London: Economist Books, 1993).

Tulgan, Bruce, *Winning The Talent War* (New York: Norton, 2001).

Weinberg, Meyer, *World Racism and Related Inhumanities: A Country by Country Bibliography* (New York: Greenwood, 1992).

West, Cornell, *Race Matters* (Boston, MA: Beacon Press, 1993).

Yang, Jeff et.al., *Eastern Standard Time* (Boston, MA: Mariner Books, 1997).

Zemke, Ron et.al., *Generations at Work: Managing the Clash of Veterans, Boomers, Xers and Nexters in Your Workplace* ( New York: AMACOM, 2000).

## Articles

Axelrod, Elizabeth et al, "The War for Talent, Part II," *The McKinsey Quarterly*, 2001.

"Best Practices for Diversity: Corporate & Candidate Perspectives," Study, Korn/Ferry, 2001.

Chambers, Elizabeth G. et al, "The War for Talent," *The McKinsey Quarterly*, 1998.

Cox, Taylor H. and Stacy Black, "Managing Cultural Diversity: Implications forOrganizational Competitiveness," *Academy of Management Executives,* 1991.

"Diversity: Making the Business Case," *Business Week,* Special Advertising Section,1996.

Hammonds, Keith, "Balancing Work and Family," *Business Week*, October 16, 1996.

_____, "Difference is Power: An Interview with Ted Childs," *Fast Company,* July 2000.

Henry, Pam, "Effective Sourcing for Diversity Candidates," *AHRMA DiversityConference Proceedings,* October 2002.

"Is the Digital Divide a Problem or an Opportunity?" Special Advertising Section *BusinessWeekOnline,* June 2002.

"Keeping Your Edge, Managing a Diverse Corporate Culture," *Fortune,* Special Advertising Section, 2001.

"Land of Plenty," Summary of the Report of the Congressional Commission on the Advancement of Women and Minorities in Science, Engineering & Technology Development, September 2000.

Levitt, Theodore, "The Globalization of Markets," *Harvard Business Review,* May-June, 1983.

McIntosh, Peggy, "White Privilege: Unpacking the Invisible Knapsack," *Peace and Freedom*, July/August, 1989.

"Protecting Growth, The Business Case for Diversity Today," Special Advertising Section, *Business Week Online,* June 2002.

Tannen, Deborah, "The Power of Talk: Who Gets Heard and Why," *Harvard Business Review,* September-October 1995.

Thomas, David and Robin Ely, "Making Differences Matter: A New Paradigm for Managing Diversity," *Harvard Business Review,* September-October 1996.

_____, "The Truth About Mentoring Minorities," *Harvard Business Review,* April 2001.

Thomas, R. Roosevelt, "From Affirmative Action to Affirming Diversity," *Harvard Business Review,* March/April 1990.

Watson, W.E., et.al., "Cultural Diversity's Impact on Interaction Process and Performance: Comparing Homogeneous and Diverse Task Groups," *Academy Of Management Journal,* 1993.

Wheeler, Michael L., "Diversity: Business Rationale and Strategies, A Research Report," *The Conference Board,* Report No. 1130-95 RR, 1995.

Wulf, William A., "The Case for Technological Literacy," *National Academies of Op-Ed Service Archive,* September 20, 2002.

_____,"Diversity in Engineering," *The Bridge,* Winter 1998.

Zachary, G. Pascal, "Mighty is the Mongrel," *Fast Company,* July 2000.

## Videos

*"Blue Eyed, Brown Eyed,"* California Newsreel

*"The Color of Fear,"* Lee Mun Wah, Stir Fry Seminars

*"Changing the Rules,"* Heim Group

*"Conflict: The Rules of Engagement,"* Heim Group

*"Diversity Management,"* R. Roosevelt Thomas

*"Gay Issues in the Workplace,"* Brian McNaught

*"Going International"* (7 part series), Griggs Productions

*"Homophobia in the Workplace,"* Brian McNaught

*"Invisible Rules: Men, Women & Teams,"* Heim Group

*"Peacock in the Land of Penguins,"* CRM Films

*"The Power Dead-Even Rule,"* Heim Group

*"Restoring Hope: Cornel West,"* NMCI

*"Sexual Harassment Awareness,"* Business Advantage

*"True Colors,"* ABC Prime Time Live

*"Valuing Differences"* (7 part series), Griggs Productions

## WEBSITES: Diversity & Multicultural Resources

www.accesscag.com

www.centerforworkandfamily.com

www.diversitybooks.com

www.diversitycareers.com

www.diversitycentral.com

www.diversityinc.com

www.diversityonline.com

www.diversityparadigm.net

www.diversityresources.com

www.getcustoms.com

www.hrpress-diversity.com

www.holidayfestival.com

www.interculturalpress.com

www.multicultural.com

www.multiculturaladvantage.com

www.ncbi.org

www.nmci.org

www.shrm.org

www.sietarusa.org

www.unesco.org/culture

www.workfamily.com

www.worldbank.org

## WEBSITES: Statistical Resources

www.acenet.edu

www.bls.gov

www.census.gov

www.eeoc.gov

www.hacr.org

www.hodesrecruitmentdirectory.com

www.hudson.org

www.nacme.org

www.nsf.gov

www.popin.org

www.popnet.org

www.prb.org

www.selig.uga.edu

www.witeckcombs.com

## WEBSITES: Resources Specific to Constituency Group

www.aarp.org

www.advancingwomen.com

www.asiandiversity.com

www.blackenterprise.com

www.gay.com

www.hispaniconline.com

www.jobaccess.org

www.nativeweb.com

# INDEX

# D

Daft, Doug, 143

Daimler Chrysler, 99

debt-to-equity ratio, 154

Delta Airlines, 93

demographics. See population

de Montaigne, Michel, 165

Denny's, 144

deregulation, 29-30

differences
    invisible, 167
    valuing of, 3, 145
    visible, 166-167

Digital Connections Conference,106

digital divide, 30-31, 174

Dillard's, 52

disabilities
    people with, 6, 22, 50

disempowerment, 121-125

diversity
    components of, 145, 185-191, 215-216
    definition of, 166-167, 184, 198
    dimensions of, 184
    in engineering, 112-113
    history of, 2-4
    initiative, 137, 177-183, 196
    necessity of, 2
    pragmatism of, ix
    scorecard, 217-220
    and social responsibility, 2-3
    training, 145, 187, 194

*DiversityInc.com,* 84, 86, 99

Dreyfus, 54

Drinan, Helen G., 177

Durand, D.E., 120

# E

Eastman Kodak, 86

economy
    global, 27, 28-31, 40-43

EEO. See Equal Employment
    Opportunity

# I

IBM. See International Business Machine

inclusion, 1, 3, 106, 118, 146, 152, 167-172, 189, 223-224

infrastructure, 182

innovation, 152-153

Inroads, 232

Intel, 151

International Business Machines (IBM), 39, 67, 93-94, 99, 100, 131, 145-146, 186

Internet, 22, 30-31, 45, 47, 48, 49, 50, 231

investment value
long term, 152, 157

Ivester, Doug, 143

# J

Janis, Irving L., 107

J.C. Penney, 54

J. P. Morgan, 86

Jackson, Rev. Jesse, 143

Jensen, Renaldo, 100

Johansen, Robert, 32-36, 127, 221

Johnson & Johnson, 54, 132

# K

Kanter, Rosabeth M., 108, 150

Katz, Judith, ix

Khosla, Vinod, 31

Korn Ferry, 123, 196-197

KMart, 53

Kraft General Foods, 27, 94, 101

Kwanzaa, 142

# L

labeling, 169

Latino. See also Mexican-American, Puerto Rican, Hispanic
as consumer, 6, 46, 264

lawsuits, 136, 140-144

leadership
behaviors, 89, 155, 183, 223-224
competencies, 89, 155, 183, 222-223
key experiences of, 225-226
role, 89, 159, 173

# N

NAACP. See National Association for the Advancement of Colored People
National Black MBA Association (NBMBA), 229, 231
NACME. See National Council for Minorities in Engineering
National City Corporation, 55
National Council of LaRaza, 197
National Association for the Advancement of Colored People (NAACP), 143, 197
National Council for Minorities in Engineering (NACME), 69
National Organization of Women (NOW), 142
National Society of Black Engineers (NSBE), 84, 231
National Society of Hispanic MBAs (NSHMBA), 229
National Study of the Changing Workforce, 93
National Urban League, 143
Native-Americans
    as consumers, 21-22, 47
NBMBA. See National Black MBA Associaiton
Neale, Margaret, 108
NSBE. See National Society of Black Engineers
NSHMBA. See National Society of Hispanic MBAs
networking, 189, 226, 232
next generation, 23, 51
*New York Times,* 93
NOW. See National Organization of Women

# O

OFCCP. See Office of Federal Contract and Compliance Program
Office of Federal Contract and Compliance Programs (OFCCP), 137
O'Hara-Devereaux, Mary, 32-36, 127, 221
organizational gatekeeping, 173
Outback, 54

# P

People with Disabilities. See disabilities
Perdue Poultry, 52
Perich-Anderson, Jajoda, 5
Peters, Tom, 181
Pfizer, 149
Philip Morris, 81, 94, 99, 101
Pitney Bowes, 86

# S

SAS Institute, 95-96
SBC Communications, 54, 99
Schering AG, 111
Schwab, 151
segmentation. See marketing
Selig Center for Economic Growth, 44
shareholder value, 153, 194
SHPE. See Society of Hispanic Professional Engineers
SHRM. See Society for Human Resource Management
Shoney's, 144
social responsibility, 2, 152, 157-158
Society for Human Resource Management (SHRM), 28, 82, 137, 177
Society of Hispanic Professional Engineers (SHPE), 229
Society of Women Engineers (SWE), 229
sourcing
    of employees, 231-233
Southwest Airlines, 96, 151
stakeholders, 162
standard of living, 30-31
Steere, William C., 149
stereotyping, 122, 124
Subaru, 54
success factors, 178-180
supplier procurement
    benefits. 81, 96-99, 158, 160
SWE. See Society of Women Engineers

# T

Target, 53
teams
    managing, 126-127, 215, 268
teenagers (See next generation)
Texaco, 142-143
Texas Instruments (TI), 85, 129, 269
Thomas, David, 4, 124
Thomas, R, Roosevelt, ix, 144
TI. See Texas Instruments
Tianguis, 53

# BIBLIOGRAPHY

American Council on Education, "Does Diversity Make a Difference?" Washington, D.C., 2000. www.acenet.edu.

Axelrod, Elizabeth L. et al. "The War for Talent, Part II." *The McKinsey Quarterly,* No.2 (2001).

2001-2002: Nineteenth annual Status Report on Minorities in Higher Education (2002). www.acenet.edu.

Bean, Linda. "Case Study in Supplier-Diversity Leadership: Renaldo Jensen at Ford." DiversityInc.com (Dec. 5, 2001). www.diversityinc.com.

*Best Practices for Diversity: Corporate and Candidate Perspectives.* Korn/Ferry. (December 2001).

*Best Practices in Achieving Workforce Diversity.* U.S. Department of Commerce and Vice President Al Gore's National Partnership for Reinventing Government Benchmarking Study (1998).

Birnbaum, P. H. et al. "Integration and Specialization in Academic Research," *Academy of Managing Journal,* vol. 24 (1981).

Branscum, Deborah. "California's Potential Workforce Woes." *Fortune* (April 26, 2002). www.fortune.com.

"Business Case for Diversity." Diversity Inc.com. www.diversityinc.com.

Caudron, Shari. "Don't Make Texaco's $175 Million Mistake." *Workforce,* vol. 76. (March 1997).

Center for Women's Business Research. "Key Facts." Washington, D. C.: 2002.

Center for Work and Family. "Facing the Facts: Changes in the Workforce." (1999). www.centerforworkandfamily.com.

Chambers, Elizabeth G. et al. "The War for Talent." *The McKinsey Quarterly,* No. 3 (1998).

Chusmir, Leonard H. and Douglas E. Durand. "The Female Factor." *Training and Development Journal,* vol. 41 (1987).

Colborn, Kate, Editor, "IBM Looks at the Future of Coporate Diversity: a Converstaion with Ted Childs." (Nov. 2001) www.diversitycareers.com.

Collins, James C. and Jerry I. Porras. *Built to Last: Successful Habits of Visionary Companies.* Harper Business (1997).

Colvin, Geoffrey. "Outperforming the S&P 500." *Fortune* (July 19, 1999).

Commission on Professionals in Science and Technology (July 2001). National Science Foundation.

Cose, Ellis. "The Myth of Meritocracy." *Newsweek* (April 3, 1995).

Cox Jr., Taylor and S. Blake. "Managing Cultural Diversity: Implications for Organizational Competitiveness." *Academy of Management Executive Journal*, vol. 5 (1991).

_____ and C. Smolinski. *Managing Diversity and Glass Ceiling Initiatives as National Economic Imperatives.* Washington D. C.: United States Department of Labor (1994).

Daniel, Cora. "Too Diverse for Your Own Good?" *Fortune* (July 9, 2001).

De Campo, Martin. "Diversity Staffing: Much More than You Think." (September 2000). www.ereexchange.com.

Digh, Patricia. "The Next Challenge. Holding People Accountable." *HR Magazine* (October 1998).

"Diversity or Diversion?" *Black Enterprise* (July 2002).

Economic Statistics by Country. www.infoplease.com.

Eisenberger, Robert et al. "Perceived Organizational Support and Employee Diligence, Commitment and Innovation." *Journal of Applied Psychology*, vol. 75 (1990).

Emerging Markets Summit V. *Institute for Executive Leadership on Diversity* (June 17-18, 2002).

Engineering Workforce Commission. Engineering & Technology Enrollment: Fall 2000 (August 9, 2001). www.aaes.org.

Ethnicity and Race by Countries. www.infoplease.com.

"Feeling Overworked: When Work Becomes Too Much." Families and Work Institute (May 16, 2001). www.familiesandwork.org.

Fiorina, Carly. Digital Connections Conference. San Jose, CA (May 4, 2000).

_____. www.hp.com.

Fletcher, Arthur A. "Business and Race: Only Halfway There." *Fortune* (March 6, 2000). www.fortune.com.

Florida, Richard. *Rise of the Creative Class* (Basic Books, 2000).

*Fortune,* Most Admired Companies. www.fortune.com.

_____, Best Companies to Work For. www.fortune.com.

_____, Best Companies for Minorities to Work For. www.fortune.com.

Frankel, Barbara. "Top 10 Companies for Supplier Diversity." Diversity Inc.com (May 22, 2002). www.diversityinc.com.

Fulford, Benjamin. "Unsung Hero." *Forbes* (June 24, 2002). www.forbes.com.

Galinsky, Ellen et al. *The Changing Workforce: Highlights of the National Study.* Families and Work Institute (1993).

Gelbar, Alene et al. "World Population Beyond Six Billion," *Population Bulletin,* Vol. 54, (March 1999).

*A Glimpse Inside of the 2001 Gay/Lesbian Consumer Online Census.* GL Census Partners. Syracuse University. OpusCommunications Group, Inc. (2001).

Gottschalk, Amy Nelson. "Shattering the Glass Ceiling: A Strategy for Survival." (June 2002) www.hrpress-diversity.com.

Graff, James L. "The Sky's the Limit." *Time* (Feb. 21, 2000). www.time.com.

Guillory, Bill and Linda Galindo. *Empowerment for High-Performing Organizations.* Innovations International (1995).

Hamel, Gary. "Reinvent Your Company." *Fortune* (June 12, 2000).

Hammonds, Keith H. "Difference is Power," *Fast Company* (July, 2000). khammonds@fastcompany.com.

Harrington, Ann. "Prevention is the Best Defense." *Fortune* (July 10, 2000).

Hayles, V. Robert. *Diversity in Corporate America.* McGraw-Hill (1996).

Henry, Pam. "Effective Sourcing for Diversity Candidates." AHRMA Diversity Conference Proceedings (October 2002).

Himes, Christine L. "Elderly Americans," Population Reference Bureau. www.prb.org.

Hoffman, Auren. "From Labor Shortage to Labor Crisis." *Industryweek.com* (January 19, 1999). www.industryweek.com.

Hubbard, Edward E. *Measuring Diversity Results,* Vol. 1. Global Insights (1997).

Humphreys, Jeffrey M. "Buying Power of the Beginning of a New Century: Projects for 2000 and 2001." *Georgia Business and Economics Conditions.* Vol. 60 (July-Aug. 2000). University of Georgia: Selig Center for Economic Growth, Terry College of Business.

"Impact of Diversity Initiatives on the Bottom Line. A SHRM Survey of the Fortune 1000." *Fortune.* Special Advertising Section (2001).

"Is the Digital Divide a Problem or an Opportunity?" *Business Week.* (2000). www.businessweek.com.

Janis, Irving L. *Victims of Groupthink: A Psychological Study of Foreign Policy Decisions and Fiascoes.* Houghton Mifflin (1972).

Kahn, Jeremy. "Diversity Trumps the Downturn." *Fortune* (July 9, 2001).

Kanter, Rosabeth M. *Change Masters: Innovations and Entrepreneurship in the American Corporation,* Touchstone Press (1985).

"Keeping Your Edge: Managing a Diverse Corporate Culture." *Fortune.* Special Advertising Section (2001).

Kelly, Eamon M. "Higher Education in Science and Engineering." National Science Foundation (April 2002). www.nsf.gov.

Kent, Mary M., Kevin M. Pollard, et. al. "First Glimpse from the 2000 U. S. Census." *Population Bulletin* vol. 56, no. (June 2000).

Kleder, Martha. "Homosexuals' Buying Power Well Above Average." C & F Report (Oct. 2001). www.cwfa.org.

Krotz, Joanna L. "Women power: how to market to 51% of Americans." *Marketing Intelligence* (2002). www.bcentral.com/articles/krotz.

"Land of Plenty: Diversity as America's Competitive Edge in Science, Engineering and Technology." Summary of the Report of the Congressional Commission on the Advance of Women and Minorities in Science, Engineering and Technology Development (September 2000).

Levitt, Theodore. "The Globalization of Markets." *Harvard Business Review* (May-June 1983).

Lukenbill, Grant. "Study Clocks Annual GLBT Spending at $340 Billion." www.gay.com.

Mehta, Stephanie M. "What Minority Employees Really Want." *Fortune* (July 10, 2002).

"Minority Buying Power in the New Century." Selig Center for Economic Growth, Terry College of Business. University of Georgia. www.selig.uga.edu.

Money Income in the U.S., 1999. U.S. Census Bureau (September 2000). www.census.gov.

Morrison, Ann. *The New Leaders: Leadership Diversity in America.* Jossey-Bass Management (1996).

Mrozowski, Jennifer. "Minority Labor Shortage Likely: Logical Result of Education Gap." *The Cincinnati Enquirer* (November 9, 1997).

*Multicultural Marketplace.* American Advertising Foundation & the American Advertising Federation (Sept, 2001).

National Action Council for Minorities in Engineering (Feb. 2001). www.nacme.org/rsch/research/data.

National Science Foundation. Division of Science Resources Statistics. www.nsf.gov.

National Study of the Changing Workforce. Families and Work Institute (1997).

Neale, Margaret A. *Research on Managing Groups and Teams*, Vol. 1. JAI Press (1998).

Nevens, Michael and Margot Singer. The McKinsey Report. McKinsey, Inc.

O'Hara-Devereaux, Mary & Robert Johansen, *GlobalWork: Bridging Distance, Culture & Time,* Jossey-Institute (1994).

Older Americans 2000: Key Indicators of Well-Being. Federal Interagency Forum on Aging-Related Statistics (2001).

Paciello, Michaeld G. "Web Accessibility: 500 Million and Growing." (March 16, 2001). www.webable.com.

Perich-Anderson, Jajoda. "A Fascination with Difference," *Futurist.com* (June 2000).

Peters, Tom and R.H. Waterman, Jr. *In Search of Excellence. Lessons from America's Best-Run Companies.* Warner Books (1982).

Pollard, Kelvin M., William P. O'Hare. "America's Racial and Ethnic Minorities." *Population Bulletin,* vol. 54, no.3 (Sept. 1999).

Principles and Recommended Practices for Effective Advertising in the American Multicultural Marketplace. AAF Foundation (2001).

"Protecting Growth, The Business Case for Diversity Today." *Business Week Online.* Special Advertising Section (June 2002).

Rayman, Paula. *Life's Work: Generational Attitudes Towards Work and Life Integration.* Radcliffe Public Policy Center. www.researchmatters.harvard.edu.

Robinson, Edward. "What About Native Americans? The Nations Original Ethnic Group Speaks Out." *Fortune* (July 12, 1999).

Roscow, Jerome M., ed. *The Global Marketplace. Facts on File.* Oxford (1988).

Rossman, Marlene. "Marketing to Women." *Multicultural Marketing: Selling to a Diverse America.* American Management Association International (1999). www.amanet.org.

_____. "Diversity in the Marketplace." *Multicultural Marketing: Selling to a Diverse America.* American Management Association International (1999). www.amanet.org.

Schepp, David. "Schepp Report: Pursuing the Elusive Pink Dollar." (July 24,2000). www.gfn.com.

Selig Center for Economic Growth. Terry College of Business. University of Georgia www.selig.uga.edu.

Stein, David et al. "Age and the University Workplace: A Case Study of Remaining, Retiring or Returning Older Workers." *Human Resources Development Quarterly* (Spring 2000).

Stein, Nicholas. "Winning the War to Keep Top Talent." *Fortune* (May 29, 2000).

Sullivan, John. "Diversity Recruting—The Compelling Case." Electronic Recruiting Daily, www.erexchange.com/public/gate.

Texas Instruments: Creating a Diversity Staffing Function. Corporate Leadership Council (October 2002). www.corporateleadershipcouncil.com.

Thomas, David A. "Cultural Diversity at Work: The Effects of Diversity Perspectives on Work Group Processes and Outcomes." *Administrative Science Quarterly* (June 2001).

_____. *Breaking Through: The Making of Minority Executives in Corporate America.* Harvard University Press (1999).

Thomas, David A., Robin J. Ely.. "Making Differences Matter: A New Paradigm for Managing Diversity." *Harvard Business Review* (Sept.-Oct 1996).

Toops, Laura Mazzuca. "Multicultural Marketing." *The Rough News Magazine* (1998).

Tulgan, Bruce. *Winning the Talent War.* W.W. Norton (2001).

United Nations. World Population Prospects: The 2000 Revisions (Highlights). Population Division. New York (2001). www.prb.com.

U.S. Census Bureau. Population Bureau. www.census.gov.

_____. World Population Profile: 1998-Highlights. www.census.gov.

U.S. Small Business Administration. Small Business Experiencing a Labor Shortage. SBA#99-45. ADVO (December 1, 1999).

U.S. Patent & Trademark Office. Patent Counts by Country/State and Year. www.uspto.gov.

Valenti, Catherine. "The Courting of the Gay Market." *The Street.com* (July 26, 2000). www.abcnews.com.

VanScoy, Kate. "The Hiring Crisis." *Smart Business from ZD Wire* (July 1, 2000).

Watson, Kumar et al. "Decision-Making Regarding Risk Taking: A Comparison of Cultural Diversity and Culturally Homogeneous Groups." *International Journal International Relations.* Vol. 16 (1992).

Wheeler, Michael L. *Diversity: Business Rationale and Strategies: A Research Report.* The Conference Board, Inc. (1995).

Witeck-Combs Communications. www.witeckcombs.com.

Women of Color in Corporate Management. Catalyst, Inc. www.catalystwomen.org.

*Women-Owned Businesses in the United Sates, 2002: A Fact Sheet.* Wells Fargo Bank, 2001. Center for Women's Business Research.

*Workforce 2020: Work and Workers in the 21st Century.* Hudson Institute (1997).

World Almanac and Book of Facts (2002).

World Bank Group. World Development Indicators. www.worldbank.org.

Wulf, Wm. A, "The Case for Technological Literacy," National Academies of Op-Ed Service Archive (September 20, 2002).

_____. "Diversity in Engineering," *The Bridge* (Winter 1998).

Yarrow, Judith. "Wrestling with the Case for Diversity." *Cultural Diversity at Work.* Vol. 10 (Nov.1997). www.diversitycentral.com.

Zachary, G. Pascal. "Mighty is the Mongrel." *Fast Company* (July 2002). www.fastcompany.com/online.

# END NOTES

1   Keith H. Hammonds. "Difference is Power," *Fast Company* (July, 2000). khammonds@fastcompany.com.

2   Thomas, David A., Robin J. Ely. "Making Differences Matter: A New Paradigm for Managing Diversity." *Harvard Business Review* (Sept.-Oct 1996).

3   Jajoda Perich-Anderson, "A Fascination with Difference," *Futurist.com*, June 2000.

4   Ann Morrison, *The New Leaders: Leadership Diversity in America.* 1996.

5   Geoffrey Colvin. "Outperforming the S&P 500." *Fortune* (July 19, 1999).

6   Morrison.

7   Michael L. Wheeler. *Diversity: Business Rationale and Strategies: A Report.* The Conference Board, 1995.

8   "Protecting Growth, The Business Case for Diversity Today," Special Advertising Section, *Business Week Online* (June 2002).

9   World Bank Group. "Global Estimates and Projections of Mortality by Cause, 1970-2015." www.worldbank.org.

10  "World Population Prospects: The 2000 Revisions" (Highlights). United Nations, Population Division: New York, 2001. www.popexpo.com.

11  U.S. Census Bureau, World Population Profile: 1998-Highlights. www.census.gov.

12  According to recent reports, the 2000 Census may have missed as many as one million Americans, at least half of whom were African-Americans and Latinos.

    A racial group is often defined by such physical characteristics as hair type, facial features and skin color. Ethnicity usually refers to social and linguistic background.

13  U.S. Census Bureau, World Population Profile: 1998-Highlights. www.census.gov.

14  Ibid

15  Alene Gelbar, Carl Haub, and M. Kent, "World Population Beyond Six Billion," *Population Bulletin*, Vol. 54 (March 1999).

16  Witeck-Combs Communications. www.witeckcombs.com.

17   *Women Owned Businesses in the U. S., 2002: A Fact Sheet.*
     Center for Women's Business Research, (2001).

18   Wheeler.

19   Jerome M. Roscow, ed. *The Global Market Place, Facts on File.*
     Oxford University Press, 1988.

20   *Workforce 2020.* Hudson Institute. 1997.

21   Digital Connections Conference. San Jose, Ca. (May 4, 2000).

22   Mary O'Hara-Devereaux and R. Johansen. *GlobalWork:Bridging Distance,
     Culture & Time.* Jossey-Bass. 1994.

23   Ibid.

24   Ibid.

25   Panel Discussion, Emerging Markets Summit V, Institute for
     Executive Leadership on Diversity. (June 17, 2002).

26   World Bank, World Development Indicators.

27   Colvin.

28   World Almanac and Book of Facts 2002.

29   China not counted due to the potential that the Chinese government has
     overstated their GDP.

30   Selig Center for Economic Growth. "Minority Buying Power in the
     New Century." www.selig.uga.edu

31   So as not to double-count women who may fall in other groups, data for
     them is not included.

32.  Selig Center for Economic Growth.

33   David Schepp. "Schepp Report: Pursuing the Elusive Pink Dollar."
     (July 24,2000). www.gfn.com.

34   Joanna L. Krotz. "Women Power: How to Market to 51% of Americans."
     www.microsoftbcentral.com.

35   In fact, marketing research indicates that some Latinos prefer ads in Spanish.
     Spanish is the predominant language in seven of the largest U.S. Latino
     markets. The key for marketers is to know which populations within the
     Latino market prefer Spanish and which prefer English.

36   High income African-Americans are turned down two and one-half times
     more often than low or moderate income whites with half the salary.

37   There are actually fifteen sub-groups, but almost 90% of Asian-Americans
     fall into these six.

38    Colvin.

39    Elizabeth G Chambers. et al. "The War for Talent." *The McKinsey Quarterly,*
      No. 3 (1998).

40    *Business Week Online,* June 2002.

41    James L. Graff. "The Sky's the Limit." *Time Magazine,* Feb. 21, 2000.
      www.time.com.

42    Net new entrants to the workforce are calculated as total entrants to the
      workforce minus those leaving it.

43    Kate Colborn, Editor, "IBM Looks at the Future of Corporate Diversity:
      A Conversation with Ted Childs." (Oct/Nov. 1998)
      www.diversitycareers.com.

44    Workforce 2020.

45    National Action Council for Minorities in Engineering.
      www.nacme.org/rsch/research/data. Feb. 2001.

46    Dr. Eamon M. Kelly. National Science Foundation. "Higher Education in
      Science and Engineering." www.nsf.gov. April 2002.

47    Engineering Workforce Commission. Engineering & Technology
      Enrollment: Fall 2000. Aug. 9, 2001. www.aaes.org.

48    National Science Foundation. Commission on Professionals in Science and
      Technology, (July 2001).

49    The mindset about aging workers in Corporate America centers on their
      perceived inflexibility and obsolescence of skills, particularly technical.
      Research seems to refute these assumptions, indicating that older workers
      are more punctual, absent less often and create lower turnover than their
      younger counterparts. Because of a high work ethic and many years in
      leadership roles, older workers bring a unique wisdom to organizations as
      role models and mentors for younger workers. Their stability and judgment
      are valuable assets in the constantly changing corporate environment. In
      their later years, they often relish assuming positions of lesser responsibility
      than what characterized their careers. Former retirees are often willing to
      engage in non-traditional work schedules, for example, working in multiple
      locations across the country during the year.

50    Workforce 2020.

51    Ibid.

52    "Keeping Your Edge: Managing a Diverse Corporate Culture," *Fortune.*
      Special Advertising Section (2001). www.fortune.com.

53. "Impact of Diversity Initiatives on the Bottom Line, A SHRM Survey of the Fortune 1000." *Fortune.* Special Advertising Section (2001).

54. Elizabeth L. Axelrod et al. "The War for Talent, Part II." *The McKinsey Quarterly,* No. 2 (2001).

55. *Business Week Online,* June 2002.

56. Kayte VanScoy. "The Hiring Crisis." *Smart Business from ZD Wire* (July 1, 2000).

57. Texas Instruments: Creating a Diversity Staffing Function. Corporate Leadership Council (October 2002). www.corporate leadershipcouncil.com.

58. Stephanie M. Mehta. "What Minority Employees Really Want." *Fortune* (July 10, 2000).

59. Alexrod.

60. Ellen Galinsky, et al. *The Changing Workforce: Highlights of the National Study.* New York: Families & Work Institute, 1993.

61. Nicholas Stein. "Winning the War to Keep Talent," *Fortune* (May 29, 2000).

62. *Business Week Online,* June 2002.

63. Axelrod.

64. Bruce Tulgan. *Winning The Talent War.* W. W. Norton. (2001).

65. Metha.

66. Center for Work and Family. "Facing the Facts: Changes in the Workforce." www.cemterforworkandfamily.com.

67. Stein.

68. Diversity Inc.com. "The Business Case for Diversity." www.diversityinc.com.

69. Barbara Frankel. "Top 10 Companies for Supplier Diversity." DiverstiyInc.com (May 22, 2002). www.diversityinc.com.

70. Ibid.

71. Linda Bean. "Case Study in Supplier-Diversity Leadership: Renaldo Jensen at Ford." DiversityInc.com (Dec. 5, 2001). www.diversityinc.com.

72. Axelrod.

73. Carly Fiorina. www.hp.com.

74   Dr. Krishna Athreya. Commission on the Advancement of Women and Minorities in Science, Engineering and Technology.. ASME Action Team Network, Seattle, WA. (October 1999). www.asme.org.

75   Carly Fiorina. Digital Connections Conference. San Jose, CA. (May 4, 2000).

76   Irving L. Janis. *Vicitms of Groupthink a Psychological Study of Foreign Policy Decisions and Fiascoes.* Houghton Mifflin, 1972.

77   Margaret A. Neale. *Research on Managing Groups and Teams.* Vol 1. JAI Press, 1998.

78   Taylor Cox, Jr. and S. Blake. "Managing Cultural Diversity: Implications for Organizational Competitiveness."*Academcy of Management Executive Journal,* vol. 5 (1991).

79   Watson, Kumar, et al. "Decision Making Regarding Risk Taking: A Comparison of Cultural Diversity and Culturally of Homogeneous Groups." *International Journal of International Relations,* vol. 16 (1992).

80   American Council on Education. "Does Diversity Make a Difference?" Washington, D. C.: 2000. www.acenet.edu.

81   Rosabeth Moss Kanter. *Change Masters: Innovations and Entrepreneurship in the American Corporation.* Touchstone Press, 1985.

82   Benjamin Fulford, "Unsung Hero," *Forbes* (June 24, 2002). www.forbes.com.

83   Colvin.

84   G. Pascal Zachary. "Mighty is the Mongrel." *Fast Company,* (July 2002). www.fastcompany.com.

85   William A. Wulf. "Diversity in Engineering." *The Bridge,* Winter 1998, pp. 8-13.

86   Ibid.

87   Ibid.

88   V. Robert Hayles. *Diversity in Corporate America.* McGraw Hill. 1996.

89   Morrison.

90   Robert Eisenberger, et al. "Perceived Organizational Support and Employee Diligence, Commitment and Innovation," *Journal of Applied Psychology.* Vol. 75 (1990).

91   P. H. Birnbaum, et al. "Integration and Specialization in Academic Research." *Academy of Managing Journal.* Vol. 24 (1981).

92   Leonard H. Chusmir and Douglas E. Durand. "The Female Factor," *Training and Development Journal*, Vol. 41 (1987).

93   Bill Guillory and Linda Galindo. *Empowerment for High Performing Organizations.* Innovations International. 1995.

94   *Women of Color in Corporate Management.* Catalyst, Inc. www.catalystwomen.org.

95   *Business WeekOnline.* June 2002.

96   Mehta.

97   Ibid.

98   David A. Thomas. *Breaking Through: The Making of Minority Executives in Corporate America.* Harvard University Press. 1999.

99   Examples include not listening, interrupting, talking too quickly, talking in slang, giving more weight to certain members' inputs over others, ignoring or prematurely rejecting ideas, not seeking clarification when a member has not been understood, etc.

100  O'Hara-Devereaux and Johansen.

101  Companies typically sponsor African-American, Asian, Gay & Lesbian, Latino and women's groups. Some also endorse groups to support Native Americans (Lucent's Luna Group is the largest), People with Disabilities, males and some religious groups. Verizon sponsors the Association of Career Employees, for employees that are age 50 and above.

102  National Study of the Changing Workforce. Families and Work Institute (1997).

103  Paula Rayman. *Life's Work: Generational Attitudes Towards Work and Life Integration.* Radcliffe Public Policy Center. www.researchmatters.harvard.edu.

104  Families & Work Institute.

105  Ibid.

106  Ann Harrington. "Prevention is the Best Defense." *Fortune* (July 10, 2000).

107  Cora Daniel. "Too Diverse for Your Own Good?" *Fortune* (July 9, 2001).

108  *Business Week Online,* June 2002.

109  Wheeler.

110  Jeremy Kahn. "Diversity Trumps the Downturn." *Fortune* (July 9, 2001). www.fortune.com.

111  Harrington.

112  Martin de Campo. "Diversity Staffing: Much More than You Think." (Sept. 2000). www.erexchange.com.

113  Kanter.

114  James C. Collins and Jerry I. Porras. *Built to Last: Successful Habits of Visionary Companies.* Harper Business. 1994.

115  Most Admired Companies Award. www.fortune.com.

116  Best Practices in Achieving Workforce Diversity. U.S. Department of Commerce and Vice President Al Gore's National Partnership for Reinventing Government: A Benchmarking Study (1998).

117  Morrison.

118  Collins and Porras.

119  Ibid.

120  SHRM Survey. *Fortune.* Special Advertising Section (2001).

121  Ibid.

122  Tom Engibous, TI's Chairman, CEO and President, is one such example. Tom is active in hosting diversity events within TI and is visible in his participation in national diversity conferences. He serves as Chair of Catalyst, a nonprofit research and advocacy organization working to advance women in business. He was recognized by the Women in Technology International (WITI) organization at its 2002 national conference as CEO of the year for his support of diversity.

123  Tom Peters and R.H. Waterman, *In Search of Excellence.* Harper & Row. (1984).

124  Edward E. Hubbard. *Measuring Diversity Results: Vol I.* Global Insights. (1997).

125  Wheeler.

126  Morrison.

127  *Best Practices for Diversity: Corporate and Candidate Perspectives.* Korn/Ferry (Dec. 2001)

128  Hubbard.

129  O'Hara-Devereaux and Johansen.

130  Morrison.

131   National Society of Black Engineers; Society of Women Engineers; Society of Hispanic Professional Engineers; Mexican-American Engineering and Science Association; National Society of Hispanic MBAs and National Black MBA Association.

132   Best Practices in Achieving Workforce Diversity. U.S. Department of Commerce.